D1683247

EP Sport Series

All about Judo
Badminton
Basketball
Conditioning for Sport
Football
Golf
Learning to Swim
Modern Riding
Netball
Orienteering
Sailing
Snooker
Squash Rackets
Table Tennis
Tennis up to Tournament Standard

ep EP PUBLISHING LIMITED
1976

Nick Whitehead in 1960, the year he ran for Britain at the Rome Olympics

ep sport

track athletics

Nick Whitehead
Principal Lecturer,
Carnegie College of
Physical Education,
Leeds

Acknowledgements

The author and publishers would like to acknowledge with thanks the assistance of the following in the preparation of this book:

John Dodd, Gordon Wilcock and other friends.

Fox Photos Ltd for the frontispiece photograph.
All-Sport Photographic Ltd for the photographs on pp. 11, 23, 41, 42, 52, 59, 61, 66, 82, 88.

ISBN 0 7158 0586 X

Published by EP Publishing Ltd, East Ardsley, Wakefield, West Yorkshire, 1976.

This book is copyright under the Berne Convention. All rights are reserved. Apart from any fair dealing for the purpose of private study, research, criticism or review, as permitted under the Copyright Act, 1956, no part of this publication may be reproduced, stored in a retrieval system, or transmitted in any form or by any means, electronic, electrical, chemical, mechanical, optical, photocopying, recording or otherwise, without the prior permission of the copyright owner. Enquiries should be addressed to the Publishers.

© N. Whitehead 1976

Text set in 11/12 pt. Photon Univers, printed by photolithography, and bound in Great Britain at The Pitman Press, Bath.

Foreword by Professor J. E. Kane

We have a very proud and envied tradition in Britain for various forms of competitive running and walking—or pedestrianism as it used to be known. The history of pedestrianism is full of the most attractive and remarkable accounts of heroic endeavours 'on foot', and these accounts must in part explain the continued interest and involvement of so many in competitive running and walking.

While this is a commendable state of affairs for any nation, it can sometimes work against the development of high-level ability. Running and walking are often regarded as 'natural' athletic events in which little or no skill is needed; and when so many are involved, the scientific approach to improvement is under-represented in the face of self-appointed experts who pass around 'hints and tips'. Dr. Whitehead has, in this book, set out in clear and simple terms the scientifically-derived fundamental information that competitive runners and walkers should know. There is, therefore, no need for anyone to be misinformed on such issues as fitness preparation, skills development and training schedules.

The author is, of course, specially qualified for the task of writing an authoritative book of this sort. He is an eminent physical educationist, coach and scholar and, most important, he was an experienced British international sprinter who rightly treasures among his possessions Olympic and Commonwealth medals.

PROFESSOR J. E. KANE
Loughborough
August, 1976

CONTENTS

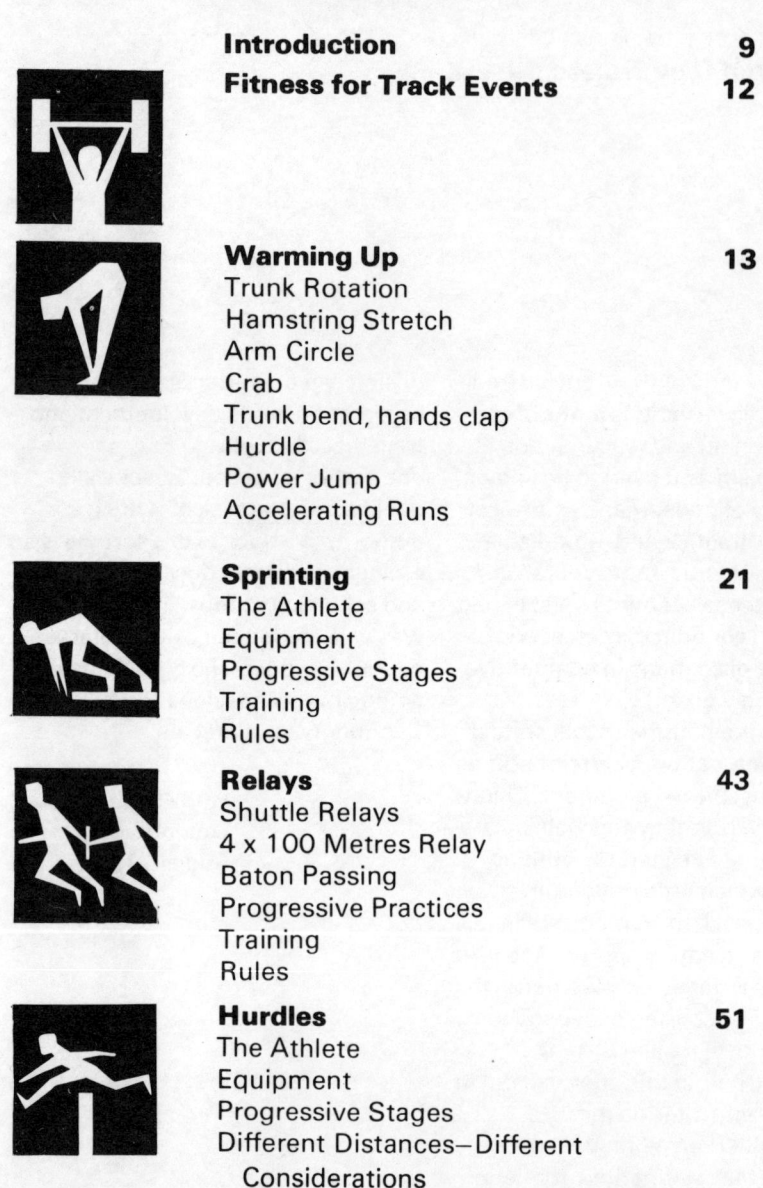

Introduction   **9**
Fitness for Track Events   **12**

Warming Up   **13**
Trunk Rotation
Hamstring Stretch
Arm Circle
Crab
Trunk bend, hands clap
Hurdle
Power Jump
Accelerating Runs

Sprinting   **21**
The Athlete
Equipment
Progressive Stages
Training
Rules

Relays   **43**
Shuttle Relays
4 x 100 Metres Relay
Baton Passing
Progressive Practices
Training
Rules

Hurdles   **51**
The Athlete
Equipment
Progressive Stages
Different Distances—Different
   Considerations
Training
Rules

**Middle Distances and
Cross-Country Running**   **65**
The Athlete
Equipment
Progressive Stages
Training – Theories
Training – Schedules
Rules

Steeplechase   **83**
The Athlete
Equipment
Progressive Stages
Training
Rules

Walking Races   **89**
The Athlete
Equipment
Race Walking Techniques
Training
Tactics
Rules

Appendix A
  Standards for schoolgirls   **104**
Appendix B
  Standards for schoolboys   **105**
Appendix C
  Standards for schoolchildren
  at Athletic Clubs   **106**
Appendix D
  Standards for Walkers   **107**
Further Reading   **108**

Introduction

Athletes and athletics coaches tend to be very technique-conscious. Coaches often seem to have a picture in their minds of the perfect athlete performing in a perfect fashion, and they direct the athletes in their care to spend hours practising a skill in an attempt to emulate that theoretical image.

Athletes seem not to mind practising these skills, possibly because the amount of effort involved is not very great compared with a hard repetition running session, or a hard weight-training session! But what both athletes and coaches ought to consider is whether all athletes *should* perform in an identical fashion—

An international athlete far too high over the hurdle, illustrating that even better athletes are not always perfect

The athletes on the far side and nearest the camera are the best stylists, but are placed only third and fourth in this race

because athletes are not endowed with identical physiques.
Shouldn't the athlete with stronger than average legs aim to use his leg strength? Shouldn't the athlete with the faster leg action aim to use his leg speed? Shouldn't the athlete with the greater arm and shoulder strength use this to his advantage?

If we examine the performances of years gone by, we will see that Jesse Owens' 1936 long jump world record of 8.13m was performed in what would be regarded today as a 'very poor style'! Yet this record stood for over thirty years despite improvements in training methods, run-up surfaces, diet, etc. Similarly, many recent world record holders cannot be regarded as prime examples of 'good style', for example Bob Hayes in the sprint and Randy Matson in the shot; but they have used their own particular abilities and strengths to the full and have beaten others who were better stylists.

This book examines each event, describes what is essential to the mechanically efficient performance of it and, beginning with simple practices, outlines progressive stages through which athletes should practise, becoming accomplished in each before they move on to the next.

Each section begins with a description of the type of athletes likely to succeed in the event named; the equipment needed is described, the progressive stages through which to practise are illustrated, training schedules for the event are itemised, and the rules for the event are summarised.
In the Appendices there appear details of performances which beginners can aspire to attain.

Training can be a long, lonely process, but there is no substitute for plain hard work. In the end, success depends on the determination of the individual

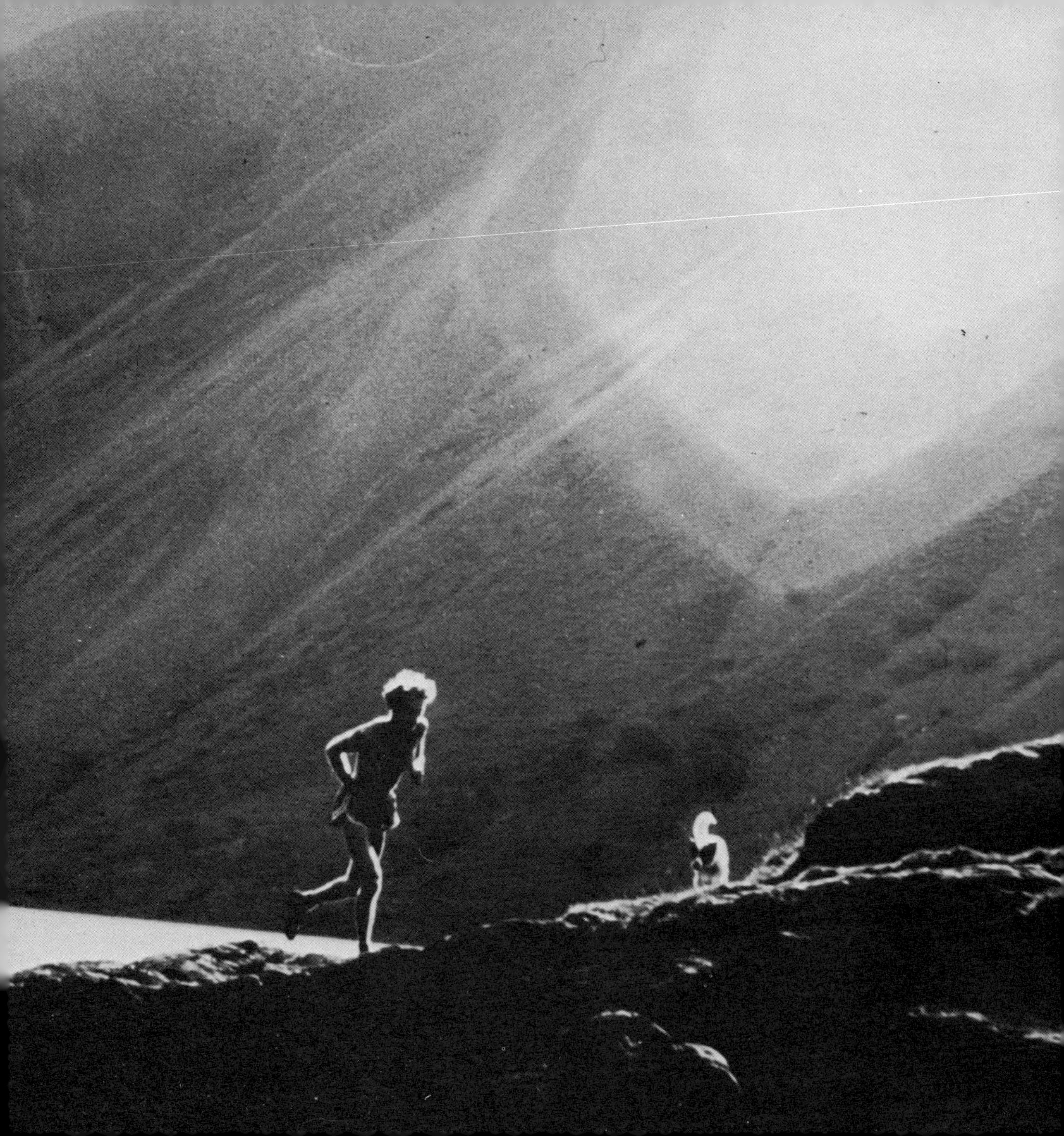

Fitness for Track Events

Often, lack of success and even injury can result from athletes practising an event before their bodies are adequately prepared for it. It could be said that they were not 'fit', even though they may have thought they were.

Much progress has been made in recent years in the acquisition of knowledge about the technique of track events, but astonishingly there is still much confusion about 'fitness' for track events. Not only is there disagreement among coaches as to the best methods of attaining 'fitness', but coaches and athletes use the term in such a fashion that they demonstrate their ignorance of the true fitness needs for the various track events. In fact, the level of fitness and training needs are different not only for each event, but for each athlete. It is easy to accept that a 'fit' water polo player is not necessarily 'fit' for basketball playing, or that a world record-holder in a track event could be regarded as completely 'unfit' in a swimming situation. Yet coaches tend to give all the sprinters in a group the same 'fitness' schedules regardless of their age and ability, ignoring the fact that some of these individuals need to apply more effort than others.

It is not possible within the confined space of this book to deal with all aspects of fitness, viz. circulo-respiratory endurance, muscular endurance, strength, flexibility and the psychological factors. Readers are therefore recommended to refer for all of this information and the construction of individual fitness programmes to *Conditioning for Sport* by this author (see p. 108).

Warming up

One of the common features in the acquiring of fitness for different track events is a group of activities known as warming up or stretching exercises. These should be carried out prior to engaging in very vigorous activity before both training sessions and competitions. Different coaches tend to emphasise different benefits to be gained from these exercises, and some athletes differ with their coaches in their estimation of how valuable the exercises are at all: nevertheless, the best athletes always warm up before they begin any explosive activity.

Some use the exercises to ensure that their muscles are gradually lengthened so that when the track session begins, they do not 'pull' or tear muscles. Others are of the opinion that the stretching exercises ensure a raising of body temperature and pulse rate with a resultant improvement in performance when they begin their track session. Yet others simply use the the warm-up period for psychological preparation for the task ahead; they perform mechanically the routine of stretching, while concentrating on a mental rehearsal of the event to come.

Whatever the purpose of the warm-up, the exercises should not be too tiring and should not be spread over too long a period of time, but they should contain a variety that will exercise most of the muscle groups in the body, including the heart and lungs, and in particular those muscles to be used in the athlete's own event. They should normally be preceded by slow jogging of up to 1,500m, and even in cold climates should not exceed a period of thirty minutes. They will vary according to the athlete's event, age, physiological make-up, the weather, and whether the race is a heat, semi-final or final.

Each coach or athlete will develop a group of exercises that have been acquired from experience. Periodically, these exercises should be reviewed and others substituted because an athlete's or coach's favourite routines can neglect important muscle groups. Moreover, using the same exercises for a period of time can result in the athlete not putting in much effort, in which case the exercises will not produce the desired effect.

There follow some illustrations and descriptions of stretching exercises that have been used by top-class athletes.

Exercise 1 (all body) Trunk Rotation

1 After the jogging, the stretching begins with an exercise that uses most of the muscle groups. The athletes, still dressed in track suits or warm clothes, bend down with hands clasped out in front of the body

2 While retaining their balance, the athletes stretch their arms as far away from the body as possible. It is a slow, sustained movement

3 Rotating around the waist, the athletes press the arms as far back behind the body as possible without overbalancing. Younger athletes do not have the strength in their abdominal muscles to be able to lean far back

4 Slowly the arms are swept far to the other side on the way down. On reaching the starting position the exercise is performed in the opposite direction. It can be repeated 6 times or more

Exercise 2 (legs)   Hamstring Stretch

1 The athletes begin with legs crossed over so that the outsides of the feet touch. It is a simple stance which children find little problem in adopting

2 Slowly they attempt to place the palms of their hands on the floor, or touch their toes with their fingers. Some athletes, like the boy on the right, will not be able to reach their toes

3 The athletes then raise their bodies and return to the starting position

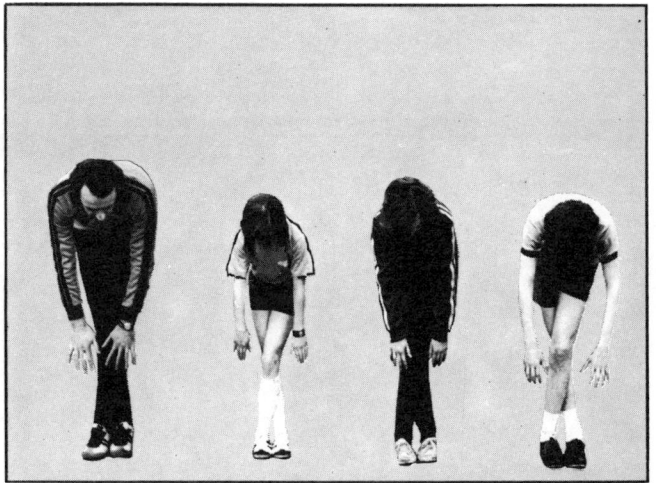

4 So that each group of hamstring muscles is stretched separately, the feet are then changed round and the exercise is repeated in a slow, stretching fashion. About 6 times with each leg in front is an average number to attempt

Exercise 3 (arms)
Arm Circle

1 With the palm of the hands on their thighs, the athletes stand lightly on the balls of their feet, with feet shoulder-width apart

2 The arms are lifted forwards stiffly, straight and very slowly until they are extended high in the air. The arms touch the ears and the body is raised onto the toes

3 Slowly, the arms are pressed backwards, and downwards. A tightness will be felt across the chest and between the shoulder-blades

4 The arms are lowered to the starting position at the same time as the body weight is taken onto the heels. The exercise can be repeated slowly about 6 times

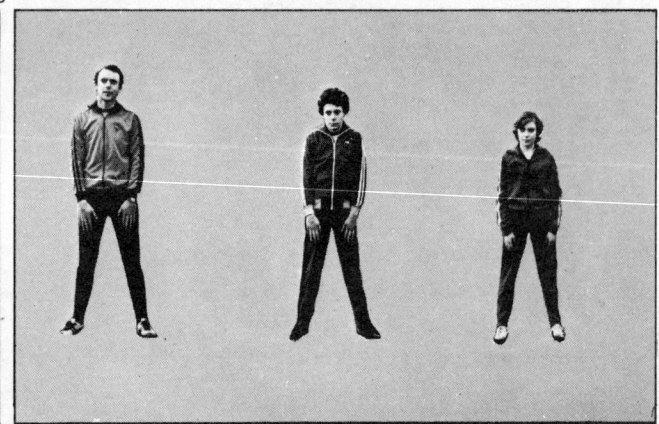

Exercise 4 (trunk)
Crab

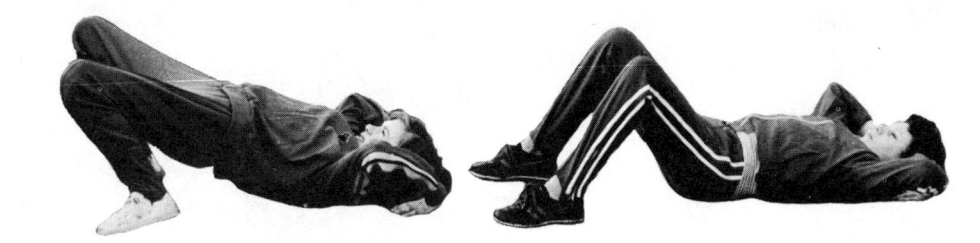

1 Many athletes struggle with this exercise; women and children tend to be more successful at it than men. The starting position is lying on the floor, hands behind the head and flat of the feet in a comfortable position under the knees

2 The objective is to get the back into as high an arch as possible. The position should be held for 2 seconds, then the body should be lowered slowly. The boy on the right is benefiting from the exercise even though he is struggling to get off the floor

Exercise 5 (arms)
Trunk bend/Hands clap

1 The athletes spread their legs apart, bend the trunk, and spread their arms wide

2 In a rhythmic fashion, they sweep their arms down to clap hands just below the head, with their arms still extended

3 The arms are then swept upwards and backwards while the trunk is bent and head facing downwards

4 Finally, the hands are clapped behind the back before sweeping down to be clapped near the floor again. A smooth action is maintained while the exercise is repeated about 6 times

Exercise 6 (legs and spine)   Hurdle

1 In a sitting position, one heel of the foot touches the buttock, the other leg stretches forward with a 90° angle between the legs. Where possible, the body is upright. Some athletes, like the boy in the middle, find this exercise difficult

2 In a slow, sustained fashion, the arms are stretched forward so that the fingers touch the toes, and the head touches the knee. The exercise is repeated with the other foot in front. A total of about 6 attempts is ample. The little girl on the right has no difficulty with this exercise

Exercise 7 (all body)
Power jump

After the slow jogging and gentle stretching, about 6 powerful jumps into the air, with an attempt to make the knees touch the chest, are useful before the training session begins

Exercise 8 (Lungs and skill)

Accelerating Runs

Before training or competition runs, in addition to stretching exercises, athletes should run distances of about 50m three or four times, gradually increasing the speed. As well as the general stretching exercises, specific practices should be carried out, i.e. sprinters should run out of starting blocks two or three times, hurdlers should run over hurdles, relay runners should practise baton passing and receiving. After these preliminaries, a period of approximately ten minutes (dependent upon the climate) should be left before the race for the athlete to lie down in a warm, comfortable spot, close his eyes and 'gather' himself psychologically in preparation for the imminent competition.

Sprinting (100, 200, & 400 metres)

'Sprinters are born and not made.'
Anonymous

It can now be revealed that the above quote was uttered by an international sprinter who hated training. He hoped that if it were to be repeated often enough, his coach would get to hear of it and would require less training from his athletes!

The truth is that sprinting is a skilful activity just like gymnastic somersaults or football kicking. Such activities must be practised constantly to retain or improve an athlete's level of ability.

The Athlete

No particular body type can be described as the ideal for a sprinter. World record holders have included the small, lithe Mike Agostini and the heavy, powerful Bob Hayes. One or two generalisations can be made about sprinters, however:
- they tend to be powerful, have long stride length and fast leg action
- some of them should try other events!

Too many athletes have been introduced only to the simple events—schools and clubs seldom attempt events which might well be more appropriate for them and their members. Many present-day 'sprinters' would achieve greater success in hurdles, triple jump, or even middle distances. One successful sprinter in Great Britain, Don Anthony, changed his event successfully in the 1950s to become an Olympic hammer thrower!

Equipment

● Competition clothing consists of vest (which *must* be worn), shorts, underwear or support, and track shoes (socks are also worn by some athletes, though tight socks should be avoided). The track shoes should be light (why carry extra weight?), and may be purchased so that the metal spikes can be replaced when worn, or for substituting indoor spikes. Spiked shoes are not difficult to get used to, they improve everyone's performance, and the expense for schoolchildren can be overcome by a physical education teacher who organises a second-hand track shoe sale annually, so that little-worn shoes which are too small can be passed down to younger athletes.

● For training and warming-up purposes, a warm track suit, old sweater, and training shoes are also essential. The training shoes should be waterproof so that during winter

Well-equipped athletes will wear track suits in training, but those who do not possess them should still train—provided they are in warm clothes

Spiked shoes are obtainable in many styles and made by various companies—the most famous and the most expensive shoes are not necessarily the best. Athletes will choose the ones which suit them best; the shoes should have permanent or interchangeable spikes on the soles

training or the warm-up prior to a race, the feet are kept dry for as long as possible.

● Starting blocks are not essential for school-children. In fact, some track meeting organisers will not permit some age groups to use them because of the time taken to fix them to the track. It is probably not in the interests of boys and girls of fifteen or less to use them because most athletes of this age start faster without blocks! Where they are used, they must be of rigid material, i.e. have no springs. A large range of blocks is available, but often it is cheaper for an athlete to make his own.

Blocks are available in many types of construction; athletes should buy a cheap, light pair or make their own. But remember that at some athletics competitions blocks provided by the organisers will have to be used

Some athletes carry tape measures with them to measure the distance of the blocks from the starting line. It is always advisable to carry large nails for fixing the blocks to the track, because there are occasions when there is a shortage of them at track meetings.

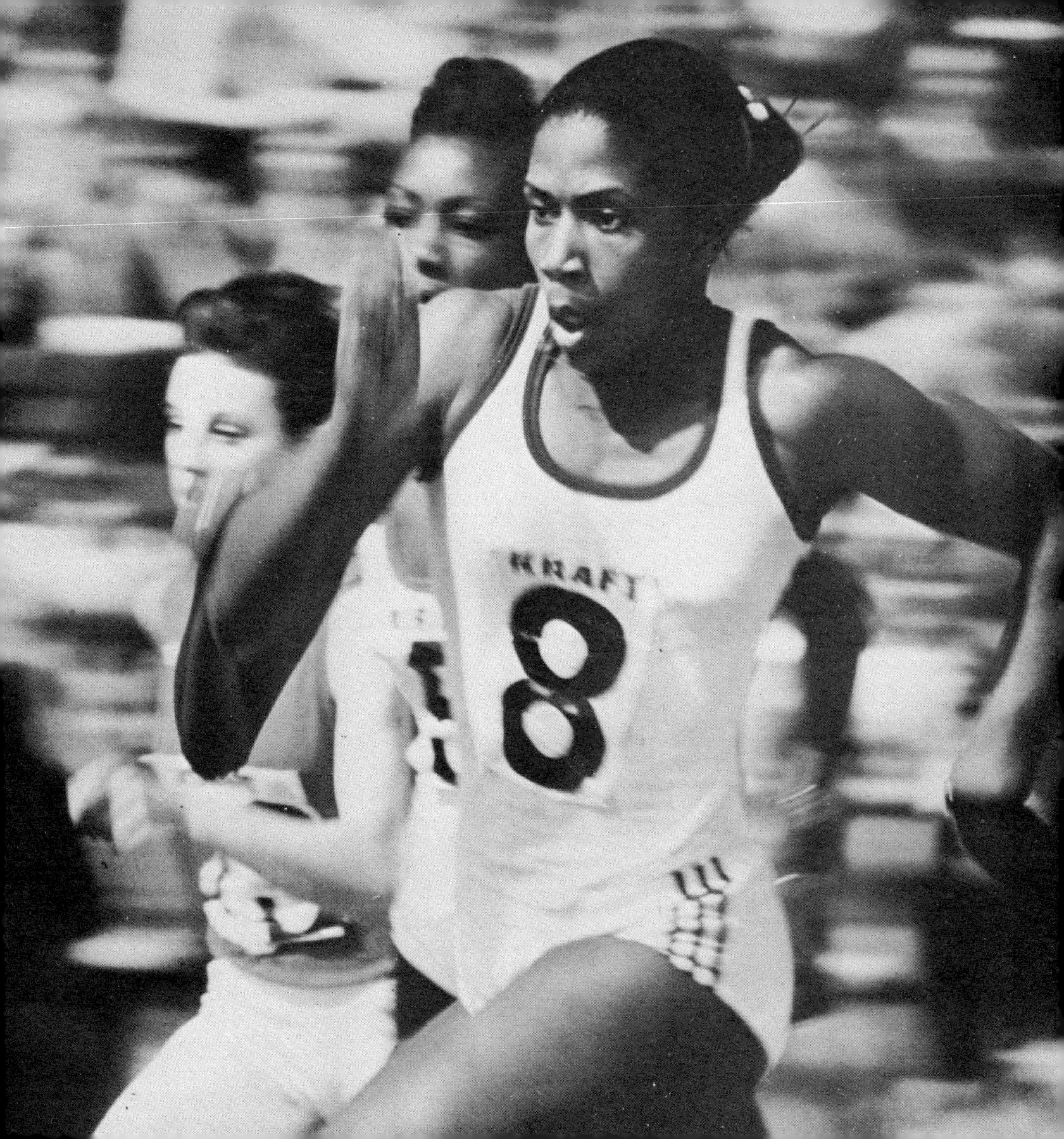
KRAFT
8

Progressive Stages

1. The Standing Start

When introducing the skill of starting to beginners, it is advisable to adopt the simple procedure of making them place one foot just behind a track starting line or the edge of a football field as though they were going to have a short race. They should then stoop a little over the leg that is in front. This style will probably be most appropriate and indeed the fastest for boys and girls up to the age of about fifteen, because until then they do not have sufficient strength in their arms to hold themselves in the crouch start.

The start should be a position from which the athletes can get away at the fastest speed, taking into account their strength and skill ability—see below

2. The Crouch Start

The transition from a standing to a crouch start is relatively easy. All that the athlete is required to do is adopt the standing start stance, lower his

rear leg until the knee touches the ground, level with the front toe, and then place his hands on the ground in front of him.

The hands should not quite be touching the starting line, and the thumbs should be pointing inwards. The front foot should be 40–50cm (16–20in) from the line and the shoulders should be perpendicularly over the fingers.

Top: the nearside athlete should have his hands behind the line, the palms should *not* be flat on the ground, his eyes should be looking just in front of the line. The athlete on the far side is demonstrating a good 'On your marks' position

Right: the girl closer to the camera should be looking just in front of the line. Because her fingers are too weak to support her weight, she places her thumb and knuckles on the ground, but they should be behind the line

The head should be held comfortably so that the eyes are looking at a point about one metre in front of the starting line. This is called the 'on your marks' position.

The next stage in the crouch start is when the starter calls 'set'. The athlete's hips are raised so that they are slightly higher than the head; the body rocks forward so that the shoulders are in front of the starting line.

Top: the nearside athlete has not raised his hips sufficiently high and his shoulders are too low

Left: the nearside athlete is looking down the track; this has the undesired effect of lowering the hips

When the gun fires, the athlete uses the arms vigorously and *runs* fast from the start, thinking neither of driving hard nor jumping.

3. The Block Start

The technique adopted in the crouch start can be more beneficially employed if holes are scratched in the cinder track where the feet are to be placed (if the track owners will permit it, that is. If they do, athletes should ensure that the holes are filled in afterwards.) Otherwise, blocks can be used and the same technique employed as in the crouch start.

Top: because of his low hips in the 'set' position and because he was looking down the track, the nearside athlete has a slower start

Right: the athlete on the far side has a faster start because of her better 'set' position

4. Improving Sprinting Style

Golfers spend hours practising and 'grooving' their strokes; tennis players do not just play tennis as part of their training, they too need to improve their techniques; but there seems to be a belief that sprinters need only to practise their start and that the remainder of the race will take care of itself. It is a fallacy to believe that 'sprinters are born' and that sprinting speed cannot be improved. Sprinting is something that will be improved if practised—but a bad sprinting style will become a worse sprinting style if nothing is done to make the style more efficient. A number of features of sprinting can be improved. For instance, if the arms are tight and limited in the range through which they drive, then automatically the legs will be synchronised into a jerky, pattering style, whereas if the arms are relaxed and driven through a wide range, the legs will be driving through a great range and the greater stride length will normally produce a faster sprint.

A number of practices can be used to improve style. First, mark out a distance of about 20–25m. After warming up, the sprinter should place his foot on the first line, then sprint beyond the second line. The number of strides taken between those lines will

These athletes are 'tight' in their muscles; this creates a jerky, shorter stride length

These two sprinters demonstrate excellent stride—with the legs behind the body straight, the knees coming up high in front, and the arms and face showing relaxation

be counted. The athlete will then be required to repeat the practice four to six times, aiming to beat the first performance, i.e. to cover the distance in fewer strides (see below).

Another practice that can assist in lengthening the stride is a pair activity. In this, one athlete has a belt or old car inner tube placed around his waist, two lengths of rope are tied to it and a second athlete holds the ropes. The objective is for the athlete in harness to run about 25m using the arms and legs vigorously, while the athlete behind gently pulls back on the harness. On reaching the 25m point, the one holding the rope goes into the harness while the other pulls back on the rope on the return run.

Furthermore, sprinters should practise alongside other sprinters. Too many athletes train alone—gold medals are won only when opposition is beaten.

The blocks on the left are pointed at a tangent to the lane line; this is correct on bend runs. The blocks on the right are badly set, pointing straight down the track

The athlete on the extreme right demonstrates a good, relaxed style. The two on the left are wasting energy with their ungainly, uneconomic styles

5. Bend Running

There are many sprinters who are able to run 100 metres very well, but who fail to achieve equal success in the 200 metres. This is not always due to their being unable to run longer distances, but often is because they do not modify their start on the bend, and do not run well around the bends because of lack of practice.

To improve bend running ability, athletes have to practise bend running! Weekly schedules should incorporate half and full-bend runs at flat-out speed. Additionally, the setting of blocks needs attention. Whereas in the 100 metres race an athlete points his blocks down the middle of his lane, in the 200 (and 400) metres, the blocks are set so that he will run out at a tangent to the bend, his first few strides taking him close to (but not touching) the inner edge of the lane.

6. Distribution of Energy

In the 100 metres race, there is insufficient time for less experienced athletes to think about anything else but running as fast as they can for the whole distance. Many would benefit from having their style 'tidied up', so that the head rolling from side to side and the body twisting were eliminated. Teachers or coaches could also ensure that the athletes adopted a more beneficial style if they were to insist on a more vigorous arm action, accompanied by a strong knee lift.

30

In both the photographs on this page, the athletes are demonstrating good, fast, relaxed running around the bend. It will be noticed that there is a tendency to lean inwards—this is automatic and should not be overstressed by coaches

Many 200 metre races are lost because of an inaccurate belief that energy should be conserved around the bend, and that the real race is down the straight. From the start of the 200 metres, the athletes should aim to get away as quickly as possible. They will find that their speed is naturally slowed down by the bend, but the aim should be to slow down as little as possible.

Nearing the end of the bend, they should consciously attempt to accelerate as fast as possible into the straight and maintain this speed by vigorous knee and arm action.

The 400 metres race involves tactics for the distribution of energy which vary considerably, being dependent not only upon the age and sex of the athletes, but also upon whether the athlete is a 400 metres runner who has progressed from 100 and 200 metres, or whether he is an occasional 800 metres runner. Varying advice has been written about the

Gritting the teeth and clenching the fists when fatigue sets in do not increase speed. The emphasis should be on a greater arm drive and knee lift

'English' and 'American' styles of running the 400 metres, viz. an even distribution of effort as opposed to a very fast first 200m. The author's opinion (and experience) is that there is a considerable amount of 'thinking' time in a 400 metres race, and so athletes should be given a number of tasks to do during the race; for example: consciously attempt a very fast first bend; concentrate on relaxation down the 'back straight'; accelerate into the final bend; over-emphasise arm drive and knee lift down the finishing straight.

The time for the first 100, 200 or 300 m of a 400 metres run is something that coaches and athletes will determine as a result of experience, and the athlete will get used to these times through practice in training sessions. The main problem is not so much the setting of these targets, but getting the athlete to adhere to them when he has the immense distractions of the race to contend with, such as natural fear, the lane draw, the known performances of the opposition, the crowd noise, the weather, etc.

Training

When a coach looks at his athletes, he will observe that no two are identical in looks. Similarly, their needs are different and their weaknesses are different, and thus different schedules are required for each athlete, though with a similar plan.

The author's preference is never to give athletes the same schedule for more than two or three weeks. Boredom can soon set in and the resultant lack of effort means that the training is not so beneficial. Another helpful hint is *not* to use stopwatches very often in training. First of all, coaches are not normally good timekeepers; secondly, wind variations and the state of the track affect times; thirdly, times in training bear no relationship to competition performances; and fourthly, poor times in training can have a bad effect on athletes' morale.

Usually, training is broken down into winter and summer schedules or off-season and during-season work. The following examples are taken from actual training programmes of good-class athletes and give an idea of the type of activities and where the emphases lie at different stages:

100 & 200 metres (MEN)
(Off-season)

DAY 1	Run 1 mile at a steady pace Do 20 – 30 minutes circuit training
DAY 2	Sprint 50m, jog 50m; sprint 60m, jog 60m Sprint 70m, jog 70m; sprint 80m, jog 80m Sprint 90m, jog 90m; sprint 100m, jog 100m Rest for 10 minutes Reverse the previous procedure, i.e.: Sprint 100m, jog 100m; sprint 90m, jog 90m Sprint 80m, jog 80m; sprint 70m, jog 70m Sprint 60m, jog 60m; sprint 50m, jog 50m
DAY 3	Rest day
DAY 4	Weight training
DAY 5	Sprint 60m from blocks five times, walking back to the start each time Rest for 5 minutes Sprint 60m five times as before Rest for 5 minutes Sprint 60m five times as before
DAY 6	'Free choice' session. Athlete can choose extra weight training session, or track session, or cross-country run
DAY 7	Rest day

100 & 200 metres (MEN)
(During season)

DAY 1	Jog 1 mile Do stretching exercises	
DAY 2	Jog to a line, sprint 80m, walk back to start Repeat five times, attempting to accelerate during the last 20m of each run Rest for 10 minutes Sprint 80m six times as before	
DAY 3	From a standing start, sprint 40m, walk 40m sprint 50m, walk 50m sprint 60m, walk 60m sprint 70m, walk 70m sprint 80m, walk 80m Rest for 10 minutes sprint 90m, walk 90m Reverse previous procedure, i.e.: From a standing start, sprint 90m, walk 90m sprint 80m, walk 80m sprint 70m, walk 70m sprint 60m, walk 60m sprint 50m, walk 50m sprint 40m, walk 40m	
DAY 4	Using starting blocks, sprint 50m five times Rest for 5 minutes sprint 50m five times as before Rest for 5 minutes sprint 50m five times as before	
DAY 5	On grass, concentrating on relaxation: Sprint 120m, walk 120m, sprint 60m, walk 60m Repeat sequence twice Rest for 10 minutes Sprint 120m, walk 120m, sprint 60m, walk 60m Repeat sequence twice	
DAY 6	Rest day	
DAY 7	Competition	

100 & 200 metres (WOMEN)
(Off-season)

DAY 1	Jog 800m Do 15 – 20 minutes circuit training	
DAY 2	Sprint 40m, jog 40m; sprint 50m, jog 50m Sprint 60m, jog 60m; sprint 70m, jog 70m Sprint 80m, jog 80m 10 minutes rest Reverse the previous procedure, i.e.: Sprint 80m, jog 80m; sprint 70m, jog 70m Sprint 60m, jog 60m; sprint 50m, jog 50m Sprint 40m, jog 40m	
DAY 3	Rest day	
DAY 4	Weight training	
DAY 5	Sprint 50m from blocks five times, walking back to the start each time Rest for five minutes Sprint 50m five times as before	
DAY 6	'Free choice' session. Athlete can choose extra weight training session, or cross-country run, or game of squash, etc.	
DAY 7	Rest day	

100 & 200 metres (WOMEN)
(During season)

DAY 1	Jog 800m Do stretching exercises
DAY 2	Jog to a line, sprint 60m, walk back to start Repeat five times, attempting to accelerate towards the end of each run Rest for 10 minutes Sprint 60m six times as before
DAY 3	From a standing start, sprint 40m, walk 40m sprint 50m, walk 50m sprint 60m, walk 60m sprint 70m, walk 70m sprint 80m, walk 80m Rest for 10 minutes Reverse previous procedure, i.e.: From a standing start, sprint 80m, walk 80m sprint 70m, walk 70m sprint 60m, walk 60m sprint 50m, walk 50m sprint 40m, walk 40m
DAY 4	Using starting blocks, sprint 50m four times Rest for 5 minutes Sprint 50m four times as before Rest for 5 minutes Sprint 50m four times as before
DAY 5	On grass, concentrating on relaxation: Sprint 100m, walk 100m, sprint 50m, walk 50m Repeat sequence twice Rest for 10 minutes Sprint 100m, walk 100m, sprint 50m, walk 50m Repeat sequence twice
DAY 6	Rest day
DAY 7	Competition

400 metres (MEN)
(Off-season)

DAY 1	Run 1 mile at a steady pace Do 20 – 30 minutes circuit training	
DAY 2	Sprint 150m, jog back to starting point Sprint 200m, jog back to starting point Sprint 250m, jog back to starting point Sprint 300m, jog back to starting point Rest for 10 minutes Reverse previous procedure, i.e.: Sprint 300m, jog back to starting point Sprint 250m, jog back to starting point Sprint 200m, jog back to starting point Sprint 150m, jog back to starting point	
DAY 3	Rest day	
DAY 4	Weight training	
DAY 5	Sprint 80m six times from blocks on a bend in the track, jogging back to the start each time Rest for 10 minutes Sprint 80m six times as before	
DAY 6	'Fartlek' run, i.e. 3 – 4 miles of jogging, striding and sprinting over a cross-country course	
DAY 7	Rest day	

400 metres (MEN)
(During season)

DAY 1	Jog 1 mile Do stretching exercises only
DAY 2	Sprint 200m in under 28 seconds Repeat twice, walking back to the start each time Rest for 10 minutes Sprint 200m in under 27 seconds Repeat twice, walking back to the start each time Rest for 10 minutes Sprint 200m in under 26 seconds Repeat twice, walking back to the start each time
DAY 3	Sprint 80m, walk back; sprint 150m, walk back Repeat sequence twice Rest for 10 minutes Sprint 80m, walk back; sprint 150m; walk back Repeat sequence twice
DAY 4	Run six times from blocks on the bend over a distance of 80m Rest for 10 minutes Run 80m six times as before
DAY 5	Sprint 100m six times, with the emphasis on relaxed running
DAY 6	Rest day
DAY 7	Competition

400 metres (WOMEN)
(Off-season)

DAY 1	Run 1 mile at a steady pace Do 15 – 20 minutes circuit training	
DAY 2	Sprint 200m, jog 200m Sprint 200m, jog 200m Rest for 5 minutes Sprint 150m, jog 150m Sprint 150m, jog 150m Rest for 5 minutes Sprint 100m, jog 100m Sprint 100m, jog 100m	
DAY 3	Rest day	
DAY 4	Weight training	
DAY 5	Sprint 60m six times from blocks on a bend in the track, jogging back to the start each time Rest for 10 minutes Sprint 60m six times as before	
DAY 6	'Fartlek' run, i.e. 2 – 3 miles of jogging, striding and sprinting over a cross-country course	
DAY 7	Rest day	

400 metres (WOMEN)
(During season)

DAY 1	Jog 1 mile Do stretching exercises only	
DAY 2	Sprint 100m, walk back Sprint 120m, walk back Sprint 140m, walk back Sprint 160m, walk back Rest for 10 minutes Sprint 160m, walk back Sprint 140m, walk back Sprint 120m, walk back Sprint 100m, walk back	
DAY 3	Sprint 100m, walk back; sprint 50m, walk back Repeat sequence twice Rest for 10 minutes Sprint 100m, walk back; sprint 50m, walk back Repeat sequence twice	
DAY 4	Sprint five times from blocks set on a bend over a distance of 60m, walking back each time Rest for 10 minutes Sprint 60m five times as before	
DAY 5	Sprint 100m five times, with the emphasis on relaxed running	
DAY 6	Rest day	
DAY 7	Competition	

Rules

There are a number of rules about sprint races of which even athletes and coaches are often ignorant. The following list of rules, though not complete, includes all the major international competition sprinting rules.

(a) Numbers shall be worn on the chest and back in sprint races.

(b) Blocks may be used in sprint races, but must be approved by the Starter.

(c) The commands prior to the start of a race are: 'On your marks' and 'Set' (in the language of the country in which the competition is held), followed by the pistol.

(d) If an athlete lifts a hand or foot from the ground before the pistol is fired, it is a false start.

(e) If an athlete is responsible for two false starts he is disqualified.

(f) During a race, athletes must remain in their own lanes.

(g) The winner is the athlete whose torso (excluding head, arms and legs) is first to be perpendicularly over the finishing line.

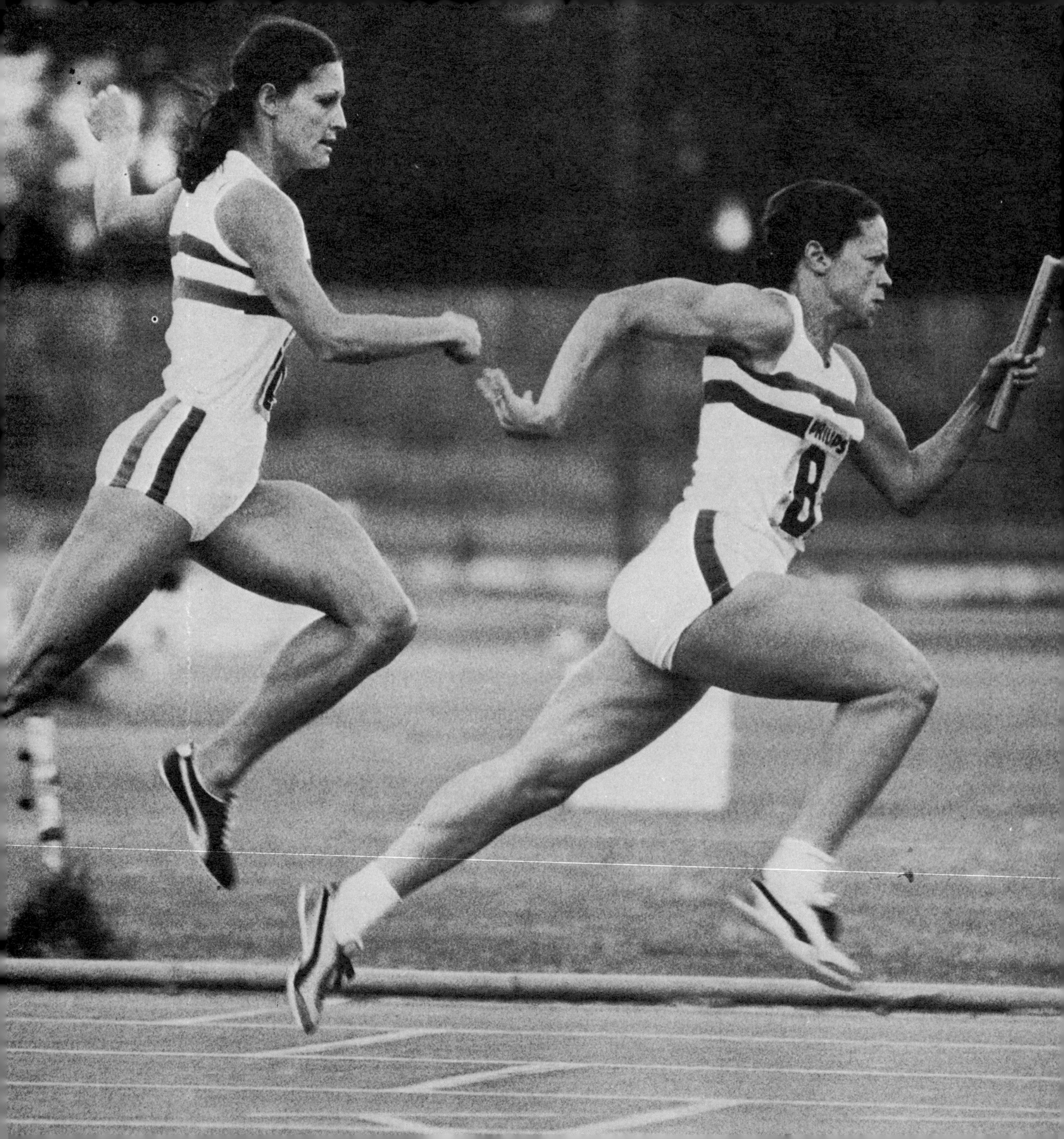
8

Relays

Shuttle Relays

Where 400m tracks are not available, much enjoyment, effort and skill may be forthcoming from shuttle relays. These can be organised in the gymnasium or on playing fields and are not confined to one team per lane necessarily, because they could be run without the use of lanes; neither are they restricted to only four athletes per team.

Shuttle relay organisation consists of lining up the teams side by side, one half of each team behind a line facing the other half of each team some distance away, as illustrated right.

On the signal from the teacher or coach, No. 1 runs to touch the outstretched hand of No. 2, who must not commence until No. 1 has crossed the predetermined line. No. 2 then runs to touch No. 3, and so on. If a baton is used, it reduces the tendency to cheat and introduces an additional skill.

Such relays could be introduced as warm-up activities at clubs and schools and could include mixed teams of men and women specialising in such different events as shot-put, high-jump, hurdles, etc.

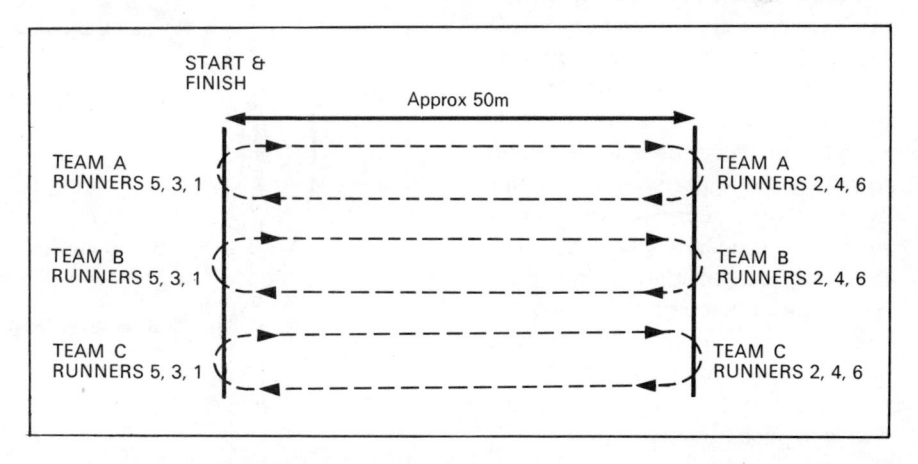

	START & FINISH	Approx 50m	
TEAM A RUNNERS 5, 3, 1		→ ←	TEAM A RUNNERS 2, 4, 6
TEAM B RUNNERS 5, 3, 1		→ ←	TEAM B RUNNERS 2, 4, 6
TEAM C RUNNERS 5, 3, 1		→ ←	TEAM C RUNNERS 2, 4, 6

RUNNER NUMBER	DISTANCE HE/SHE RUNS	DISTANCE HE/SHE CARRIES THE BATON	SPECIAL SKILLS NECESSARY
1	100 metres	100 metres	Must be a good starter Must be able to run around a bend
2	120 metres	100 metres	Must be able to receive baton in left hand Must be a good 'straight' runner
3	120 metres	100 metres	Must be able to receive baton in right hand Must be a good 'bend' runner
4	120 metres	100 metres	Must be able to receive baton in left hand Must be a good 'straight' runner Must not give in under pressure

The details given refer to an ideal situation in which the baton is received half way through the relay box at all exchanges. Even so, it will be noticed that no two 'legs' are alike in the distance run and in the responsibility of the runner, and selecting a 4 x 100m relay team therefore requires a great deal of thought before the practising begins.

4 × 100 Metres Relay

Throughout the world there is a mistaken belief that all that is required to create a successful relay team is to put together the first four athletes from a school, club, or country's 100 metres championships and spend a small amount of time on baton practice.

Some team selectors make a gesture to signify their greater understanding by including one or two 200 metres runners. But generally not enough time is spent considering what the needs are for each particular leg of the relay. The diagram on the right outlines the different characteristics of each leg, and above are details of the needs of each runner.

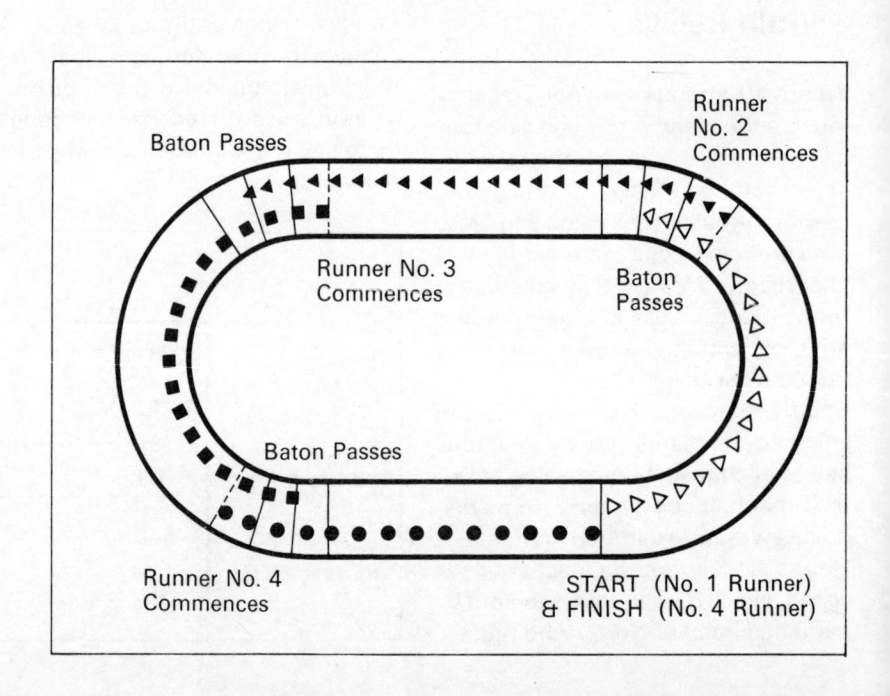

Baton Passing

Primary School Method

A simple method of passing the baton is the one illustrated above. The outgoing runner presents a target with his left arm for the incoming runner to place the baton in. On receiving the baton, the outgoing runner changes it to his right hand, then continues running to present the baton in a similar fashion to the next runner.

Using this method, the outgoing runners simply stand inside the relay box and start jogging with the head turned to be able to see that the incoming runner does not stop through fatigue. A check mark should be placed on the track a 'safe' distance before the box, dependent upon the ages and speed of the athletes. When the incoming runner reaches the check mark, the outgoing runner sets off. The emphasis in this style is on receiving the baton with little risk of disqualification.

High School Method

Older athletes who have had some experience of baton work may progress to a faster style of baton pass. In this method, the check marks are placed farther away from the outgoing runner. When the incoming runner reaches the check mark, the outgoing runner runs away as fast as possible, not looking back, and extends his left hand back to await an upsweep pass from the incoming runner's right hand.

The baton is then changed to the right hand ready to pass to the left hand of the next runner. With this method, the stretching back of the hand means that the incoming runner does not have to go as near to the outgoing runner, and so a faster relay results.

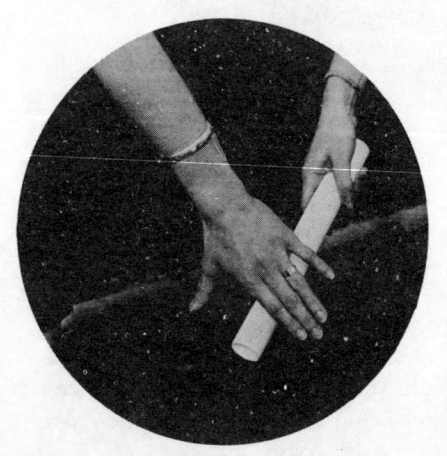

Downward Sweep Pass

Well-constructed relay teams can graduate to a method in which there is a higher element of risk of disqualification, but which gives a much faster overall speed of the baton. In the downward sweep method, the first runner holds the baton in the **right** hand, the second runner starts to the right of the lane and when runner no. 1 reaches a predetermined check mark, no. 2 runs off as fast as possible. At the seventh stride he puts back his left hand, palm uppermost, and no. 1 sweeps the baton down firmly into his left palm. No. 2 keeps the baton in his left hand and passes downwards to the **right** hand of no. 3, who runs around the bend and passes downwards to the **left** hand of no. 4. By not changing hands, there is a considerable saving of time, and an overall faster time is normally recorded.

Upward Sweep Pass

The downward sweep technique of not changing the baton from one hand to the other can be employed using an upsweep. However, the athletes must make sure that they to give plenty of baton to the outgoing runner, otherwise time could be wasted having to adjust the baton in the hand.

Visual Technique

This method is often used in 4 × 400 metres relays where the athletes are tiring towards the end of the race, and sometimes in 4 × 100 where children or unreliable athletes are used.

Progressive Practices

1. Whatever method is employed, athletes must first be introduced to it by working in twos at walking pace. The athlete at the back places the baton in the desired fashion into the hand of the athlete in the front, then walks briskly to the front to receive the baton from his partner. This continuous passing has the added objective of giving practice at receiving in both hands.
2. The next stage is to complete the passing routine at a jog. Here the additional difficulties of keeping the receiving arm still while jogging and of handing over the baton to a possibly moving target are introduced.
3. The speed of the exchange practice can be increased with all athletes having practice of receiving and passing the baton using alternately left and right hands. These practices enable athletes to discover whether they are better at receiving or passing a baton, and which of their hands is the most adept at this skill.
4. As soon as the baton passing has been practised at speed, it must be remembered that the baton must also be received within a limited area—the 'take-over zone' of 20m. To ensure that this is carried out accurately, 'check marks' need to be used. These are marks placed on the track (on cinder tracks, a scratch mark made by the athlete's spiked shoes; on all-weather surfaces, a chalk mark or a strip of adhesive tape); when the mark is reached by the incoming runner, the outgoing runner knows that he must start running (above).

The check-mark of these athletes should be extended to save time in the passing of the baton

The athlete will be given a number of foot lengths to try by his teacher or coach. If, for instance, it is decided to use fifteen foot lengths as a check mark, a baton pass will be attempted at full speed using that distance check mark. If the incoming runner passes or comes too close to the outgoing runner, then the check mark needs to be extended to perhaps twenty foot lengths, and another attempt made. If on this occasion the incoming runner does not catch the outgoing runner, then the check mark is reduced to, say, eighteen foot lengths and so on, until the baton pass is successfully carried out.

The check-mark of these athletes is too far away, hence the unsuccessful attempt to pass the baton before the end of the relay box

5. Check mark distances are calculated after much trial and error. The most conveniently accurate method of measuring them is for the outgoing runner to measure from the beginning of the take-over zone in foot lengths towards the athlete who is going to pass to him.

49

Training

Baton passing must be practised frequently, and at full speed. It is no use the incoming runner running in slowly and then accelerating over a short distance; this creates inconsistency because during a race the incoming runner will have run over 100m by the time he reaches the take-over zone. Training runs should require the incoming runner to run at least 50–60m.

Additionally, there must be consistency in the speed at which the outgoing runner starts his run, and so his starting position should be as near to a sprint race 'set' position as possible. See the two examples above.

Adult athletes will probably place one hand on the floor for support; those who do not have strong fingers will not be able to hold that position, but will nevertheless adopt a 'crouch' stance. They will stand to one side of the lane, i.e. if they are to receive the baton in the left hand, they will stand to the right of their lane. Their bodies will point forwards, only the heads being turned to look at the checkmark.

Practices should take place at different parts of the track, so that some baton passing occurs on the bend of the track, some on the straight. Finally, once a team has been selected, they need to practise **over the full distance with opposition.**

Rules

(a) In 4 × 100 and 4 × 400 metres relays, there must be four runners who must run the distance specified.
(b) The baton must be passed and not thrown from one athlete to the other.
(c) The baton must be passed within the 20m take-over zone.
(d) If the baton is dropped, the athlete who drops it must pick it up, and in doing so must not impede other athletes in the race.
(e) The usual rules relating to sprinting apply, viz, use of starting blocks, starter's commands, the necessity of athletes staying in their own lanes, the judging and timing of athletes.
(f) Contravention of the rules leads to the whole team being disqualified.

Hurdles

Though these athletes are working vigorously, only the man second from the left is performing in a reasonably good hurdling technique. All are far too high over the hurdle

Hurdling can be an event in which athletes run as fast as possible between the hurdles and leap over the barriers in a variety of ungainly styles. There are a number of reasons why inexpert hurdling is carried out in this fashion:
- lack of knowledge of hurdling technique
- lack of mobility in the hip joint and spine
- fear of the obstacles.

At top level, these factors must be overcome; but at school level, hurdling can still be an enjoyable, different challenge to those children who will never be able to become good hurdlers.

The Athlete

Hurdlers must essentially be tall, long-legged, fast, supple, powerful athletes. There have of course been exceptions, such as the Great Britain Olympic 400 metres hurdler Peter Warden, who was only about 5′ 6″ tall, and the Australian woman Olympic medallist Pamela Ryan. But such smaller athletes need to work harder to overcome their height disadvantage. In the past, Olympic hurdlers have included athletes such as Vic Matthews of Great Britain, who was relatively slow over the 100 metres sprint race, but whose exceptional ability over the hurdles compensated for his lack of speed. Nowadays, however, top-class hurdlers such as Alan Pascoe are also among the best sprinters in the country.

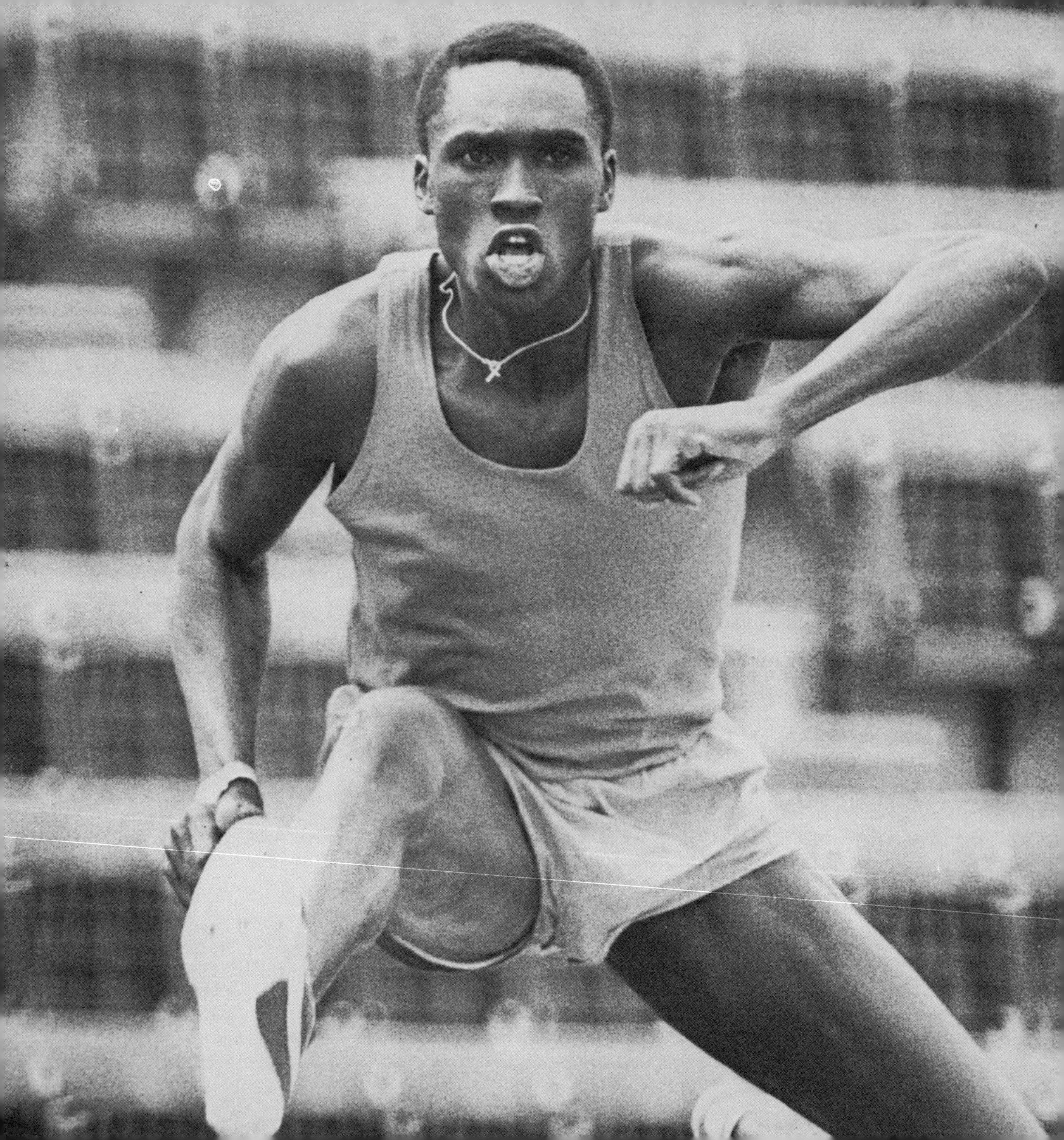

Equipment

No personal equipment is needed additional to that of a sprinter. But as men and women of different ages race over different heights of hurdles with different distances between, it is essential to know these to ensure that athletes are training for the correct event:

	Race Distance	Hurdle Height	No. of Hurdles	Distance from Start to 1st Hurdle	Distance Between Hurdles	Distance from last Hurdle to Finish
GIRLS AND WOMEN						
Age						
13 & 14	70m	68cm	8	11m	7m	10m
15	75m	76cm	8	11.5m	7.5m	11m
16 & 17	80m	76cm	8	12m	8m	12m
18	100m	84cm	10	13m	8.5m	10.5m
18	200m	76cm	10	16m	19m	13m
18	400m	76cm	10	45m	35m	40m
BOYS AND MEN						
Age						
13	70m	68cm	8	11m	7m	10m
14	75m	76cm	8	11.5m	7.5m	11m
15	80m	84cm	8	12m	8m	12m
16 & 17	100m	91.4cm	10	13m	8.5m	10.5m
18	110m	99cm	10	13.72m	9.14m	14.02m
19	110m	106.7cm	10	13.72m	9.14m	14.02m
Also for Age 17+	200m	76.2cm	10	18.29m	18.29m	17.10m
	400m	91.4cm	10	45m	35m	40m

The older type of hurdle has weights supplied separate from the hurdle. They are screwed on to the appropriate spot on the hurdle leg, dependent upon the hurdle race for which it is being used

The modern 'international' type hurdle has the weights built into the leg. They can be moved forwards and backwards to ensure the correct 'toppling force'

The hurdles must be weighted so that it takes a force of 3 kg to overturn them in races for 16-year-olds and under, and 4 kg for 17-year-olds and above. The weights may be separate from the hurdle or built in.

This static 'hurdling position' is useful only to ascertain that the athlete on the left is very stiff in legs and spine, the centre athlete is quite flexible, whereas the lady on the right is also stiff in the spine. It does *NOT* improve their hurdling ability, no matter how often they practise it

Progressive Stages

Teachers and coaches often fail to realise what hurdling really is. They tend to set out one or two hurdles and require children or athletes to get over them, regardless of the fact that even to adults the hurdle can appear to be a terrifying obstacle. Other teachers and coaches tend to overemphasise the 'hurdling position', or what the coach assumes the athlete's pose should be when he is going over the hurdle. Thus the athlete is required to practise this position while sitting on the ground or while walking around.

This is another exercise which is useful as a flexibility aid, but *NOT* as a replacement for actual hurdles practice

It would be better if hurdling were to be regarded as a race in which an athlete sprinted as fast as he could from A to B whilst clearing hurdles en route. Then from the beginning the emphasis would be on speed over a distance, and not artificial poses or the clearing of one hurdle.

1. First Introduction

Beginners should be confronted with a number of different lanes in which strips of wood, chalk marks or some other indications present 'obstacles' to the athletes' progress. In one lane the 'obstacles' will be close together, then adjacent lanes will contain a gradually increasing distance between the 'obstacles', as shown.

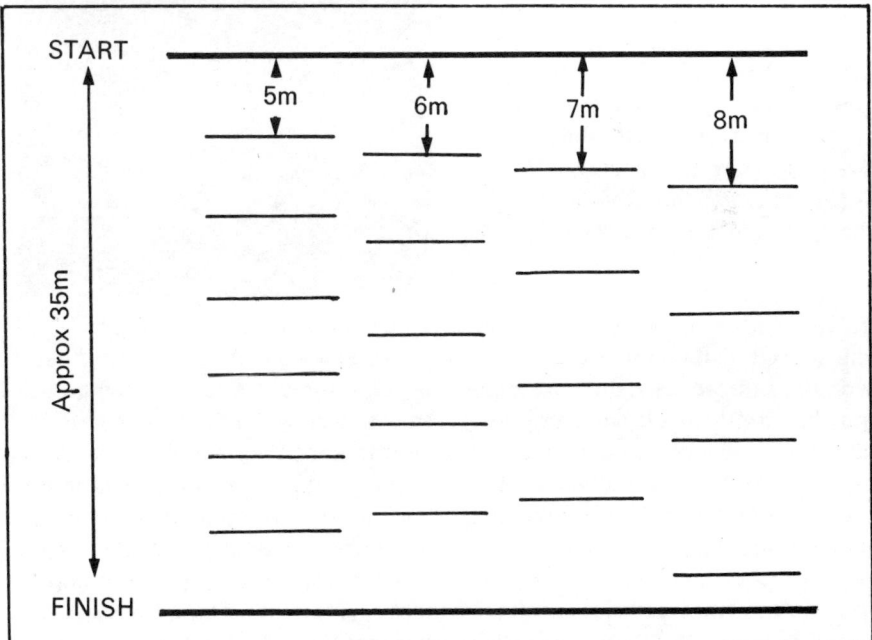

The objective is for all the athletes to start in the lane with 5m gaps and attempt to run over the lines in a regular pattern of running with the same foot stepping over the line each time. By moving up to the 6 or 7m lanes, the long-legged athletes will finally find a lane that suits them, and the group will be divided among the lanes according to their leg-length, stride-length, or athletic ability. Gradually they must increase their speed, at which time they might find the need to move up to the next lane.

2. When the teacher or coach is convinced that all the athletes are working satisfactorily, the next stage may be introduced. Using bamboo canes or similar pieces of wood placed across bricks, skittles, small waste paper bins or similar objects that are about 20–30cm high, the same practice can continue, except that this time the obstacles are slightly higher.

The same emphasis will be on covering the distance as fast as possible with the same foot stepping over the obstacle each time. Some will start to knock the wood off its supports, in which case they need to go back to the next lane down. After more practice with the teacher or coach emphasising good sprinting technique, another stage will be necessary.

3. In the next stage, the teacher or coach simply raises the height of the cane to approximately 40–50cm, and practice continues. Again, some might need to go back to another lane, and those who are not lifting their knees high in the normal sprinting position will be knocking the cane from the support. However, there should still be no jumping over the obstacle.

Should the athletes be young or small there might be a need to go on to the next stage soon—that is if the majority are now beginning to knock the cane down while adopting a normal sprinting action.

4. Introduction to Hurdling

The first thing to do at this stage is to show the children or athletes the safe and the dangerous aspects of hurdling. It will be pointed out that the hurdle must always be encountered from the front; that is,

Right: the hurdling action is the sprinter's high knee lift action

Far right: the rear leg comes through with the knee and toe pointing outwards

where the two bases of the hurdle are pointing. If the hurdle is accidentally touched while hurdling in this direction, it will simply fall to the floor, whereas if the athlete hits a hurdle because he has been foolish enough to go over it in the wrong direction, then the hurdle will increase in height and the athlete could be hurt.

Next it is demonstrated how the first part of the sprinting action, a vigorous raising of the front knee, can apply over the hurdle. The rear knee, however, cannot come through high otherwise it would hit the hurdle, so it has to point outwards. Similarly the rear toe cannot point down, so it too points outwards.

With beginners, the teachers will have to allow them to 'get the feel' of the movement before they attempt to go over at full speed

The athlete going in the correct direction will simply knock the hurdle down if he hits it

The athlete going in the wrong direction will get hurt if he hits the hurdle

57

PATH OF THE CENTRE OF
GRAVITY OF A POOR HURDLER

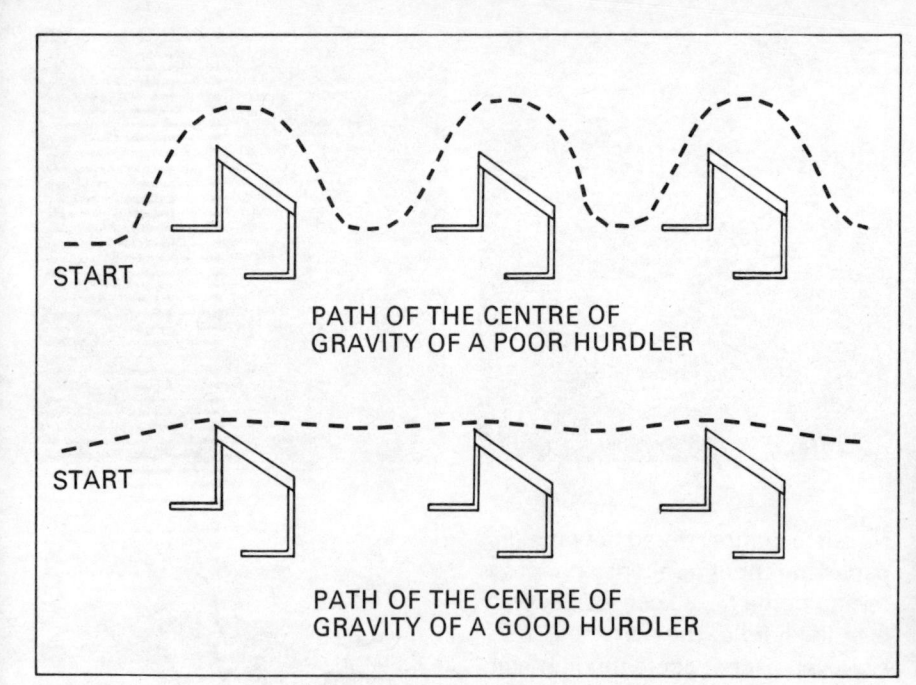

PATH OF THE CENTRE OF
GRAVITY OF A GOOD HURDLER

An athlete practising the hand to opposite toe, knee touching chin, chest along thigh position

This demonstration can take the form of the teacher or coach stepping over the hurdle slowly for all to see and the athletes doing likewise. But at this time it must also be pointed out that if athletes go over hurdles with the body upright, then their centres of gravity cover too great a distance and they will therefore take a longer time to complete the race.

The athletes should practise going over one hurdle to begin with at its lowest height (this is usually 76cm, but sometimes 60cm or 68cm), remembering the rear leg action and attempting to keep the body low.

5. After the initial practice over one hurdle, the athletes can be asked to look at their friends so that they can appreciate the good and bad points of technique. At the early stage, they will tend to jump because of fear of hitting the hurdle with their knees or feet. With the growth of confidence, they will go over at a lower height and can then be coached further.

At this stage, however, some will obviously stand out as non-hurdlers. Teachers or coaches should consider the advisability of keeping such athletes on the previous practices of 'hurdling' over canes, rather than continue to force them to jump over an obstacle which they find frightening.

6. **Further coaching points include:**

- attempting to touch the leading toes with the opposite hand
- attempting to touch the leading knee with the chin
- attempting to lay the chest along the leading thigh.

7. The next stage will be to introduce a second hurdle so that not only does the athlete clear one hurdle, he now has to think about a pattern of three strides between this and the next hurdle. See the diagram opposite.

8. Within a short period of time, yet further hurdles must be introduced because otherwise athletes can be preoccupied with hurdle clearance instead of with getting from start to finish as fast as possible.

9. Practice must then be given from a starting line to the first hurdle because of the difficulty encountered by some who might have to change their feet around at the start. This might be necessary in order to accommodate a pattern of strides that will lead the athlete to the first hurdle with the correct leg in front. After this point it is simply more practice at hurdling, more sprinting, more suppling of the hips and spine and more strength work which are required.

Different Distances—Different Considerations

Though a number of world-class hurdlers are equally effective over both 110 metres and 400 metres (e.g. Alan Pascoe and David Hemery), the majority of hurdlers are normally either short *or* long hurdles race specialists. Teachers and coaches should therefore be aware of the different essentials required in the various hurdles races.

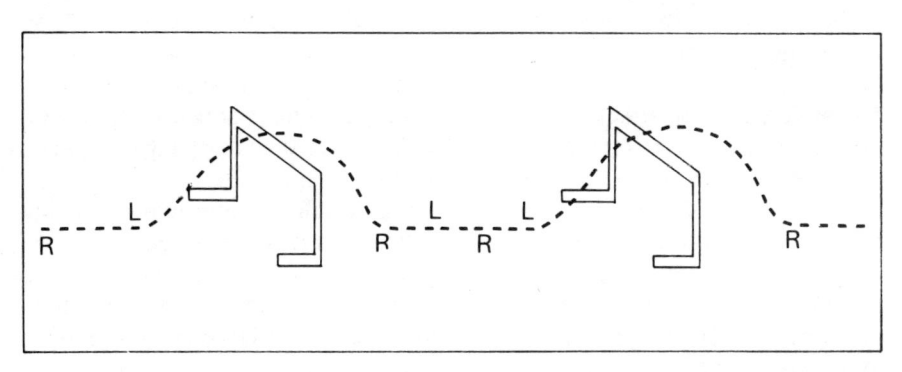

Left: women's hurdling technique is similar to men's in many ways; the principles of efficiency of effort apply, and the women's normal extra flexibility is an advantage, but these three athletes also demonstrate that women can make the same mistakes as men—too high over the hurdle and arms all over the place!

Below is a good demonstration of an athlete 'attacking' a hurdle—despite the construction of it. In this photograph, taken in the 1940s, the athlete is not too high over the hurdle when one considers the injury he would sustain if he hit it!

Girls and Women

The only Olympic hurdles event is the short hurdles race, i.e. 100 metres. Internationally, 400 metres races have been introduced, and in some countries 200 metres hurdles events are included in their championships. But until the longer events become more popular, it suffices to state that hurdling emphases and techniques for women resemble those in the men's short events. Women who are presently running 200 and 400 metres flat races could attempt the 200 and 400 metres hurdles events because there is a great deal of room for improvement in these events.

Boys and Men

Short hurdle events require precision at the start of a race. Normally about eight strides are taken to the first hurdle, though some tall athletes manage to complete the distance in seven strides. There must be much practice with starting block spacings and different feet in front at the start to achieve the ideal pattern of strides to the first hurdle. This part of the race needs fast, vigorous arm and leg action.

The athlete should 'attack' the first hurdle, driving towards it with a vigorous body dip and pulling the rear leg through quickly. In the senior events, he will normally take off about 2m before the hurdle and land 1·2m the other side of it. Thus with a vigorous arm action and stride length of over 2m, he can cover the distance between the hurdles adequately. When they complete the last hurdle, athletes are slowing down and tend to consider that the race is over. They should go vigorously for the finishing line with arms and knees and not simply dive the last few metres with chins forward and arms flying behind them.

Long hurdle events require the ability of the athlete to run longer than the hurdle distance at a fast pace. A guide is the fact that good hurdlers run the 400 metres hurdles only 3–4 seconds

At the end of a hurdles race, the three women athletes below demonstrate reasonably good, relaxed finishing technique. Right, the winner's pose is echoed by top-class sprinter Donna Murray

slower than they run the 400 metres flat race.

In the approach to the first hurdle, an athlete should practise a consistent pattern of strides, to which he will always keep in training and competition.

As the longer races have lower hurdles than the 110 metres race, the amount of body-dip is less and the emphasis is not so much on a vigorous movement as on a fast clearance.

Between hurdles an odd number of strides is usual, but world-class performers practise clearances with both legs so that when fatigue sets in they can change their pattern of strides if necessary.

The run-in from the last hurdle is very important in the longer races because of the greater distance there is to the finishing line. The athlete should try not to 'tighten up' and should attempt to maintain the rhythm used between the hurdles.

Training

Hurdlers could fool many a bystander into believing that they were training hard by simply going over the hurdles often (but slowly), by laboriously repeating the 'hurdle position' on the floor, by 'high-stepping' over hurdles and by employing high-kicks and other hip mobility exercises. The better performers, however, work hard in training and do not play around with useless, unrelated skills. Because of the range of abilities, differing age-groups, and different hurdle heights and distances, it is difficult to suggest an 'average' man's or woman's training schedule, but what can be illustrated are the kind of activities in which the athletes can be participating in winter and summer.

Short Hurdles Race (MEN)
(Off-season)

DAY 1	30-minute Fartlek	
DAY 2	1 mile run and circuit training or weight training	
DAY 3	Run 80m over hurdles six times Run 100m with no hurdles six times	
DAY 4	Weight training	
DAY 5	Train hard on track with sprinters	
DAY 6	Using a crouch start,	go fast over 1 hurdle (hurdling) go fast over 2 hurdles (hurdling) go fast over 3 hurdles (hurdling) go fast over 4 hurdles (hurdling) go fast over 5 hurdles (hurdling) go fast over 6 hurdles (hurdling)
	Rest	
	Using a crouch start,	go fast over 6 hurdles (hurdling) go fast over 5 hurdles (hurdling) go fast over 4 hurdles (hurdling) go fast over 3 hurdles (hurdling) go fast over 2 hurdles (hurdling) go fast over 1 hurdle (hurdling)
DAY 7	Rest day	

Short Hurdles Race (MEN)
(During season)

DAY 1	Jog, do stretching exercises and work on faults
DAY 2	Train hard with sprinters on track
DAY 3	Run over six hurdles six times Run 50m six times
DAY 4	Train with sprinters from blocks over 60m; repeat five times Run from blocks over six hurdles; repeat four times
DAY 5	Short sprint session
DAY 6	Rest day
DAY 7	Competition

Short Hurdles Race (WOMEN)
(Off-season)

DAY 1	20-minute Fartlek	
DAY 2	Run 1 mile Do circuit training	
DAY 3	Run 60m over hurdles five times Run 80m without hurdles five times	
DAY 4	Do weight training	
DAY 5	Train with sprinters on track	
DAY 6	Using a crouch start, go fast over 1 hurdle (hurdling) go fast over 2 hurdles (hurdling) go fast over 3 hurdles (hurdling) go fast over 4 hurdles (hurdling) go fast over 5 hurdles (hurdling Rest for about 7 minutes Using a crouch start, go fast over 5 hurdles (hurdling) go fast over 4 hurdles (hurdling) go fast over 3 hurdles (hurdling) go fast over 2 hurdles (hurdling) go fast over 1 hurdle (hurdling)	
DAY 7	Rest day	

Short Hurdles Race (WOMEN)
(During season)

DAY 1	Light day, working on technique faults
DAY 2	Train hard on track with sprinters
DAY 3	Run over five hurdles; repeat five times Run 50m six times
DAY 4	Train with sprinters from blocks over 60m; repeat five times Run from blocks over six hurdles; repeat four times
DAY 5	Short sprint session
DAY 6	Rest day
DAY 7	Competition

Long Hurdles Race (MEN)
(Off-season)

DAY 1	40-minute Fartlek
DAY 2	Weight training or circuit training
DAY 3	Run over five correctly-spaced hurdles; repeat four times, working on approach run and stride pattern Run 200m four times
DAY 4	Weight training
DAY 5	Train hard with 400m flat race men
DAY 6	Train with high hurdlers or run over five hurdles twice
DAY 7	Rest day

Long Hurdles Race (MEN)
(During season)

DAY 1	Jog, do stretching exercises, work on faults
DAY 2	Train hard with 400m flat race men
DAY 3	Run over five correctly-spaced hurdles; repeat three times Run 150m three times Run 60m three times
DAY 4	Train from blocks around the first bend, 110m, six times Run from blocks over five hurdles; repeat four times
DAY 5	Short sprint session with 200m and 400m athletes
DAY 6	Rest day
DAY 7	Competition

Rules

(a) Athletes must go **over** the hurdles (some tend to swing a leg around the side of a hurdle).
(b) If the hurdles are weighted, all can be knocked down; otherwise an athlete is disqualified if he knocks down three or more hurdles.
(c) Athletes must keep in their own lanes.

The athlete on the left of this photograph is liable for disqualification for impeding the other athlete's progress

(d) The usual rules about start and finish in Sprints apply equally to hurdles races.

Middle Distances and Cross-Country Running

'The secret of running is not to get out of breath.'

ANON

To the layman, distance running must appear to be the least complicated form of track and field athletics. There is no aerodynamic equipment necessary, as in the throwing events; no resorting to clandestine use of anabolic steroids in order to develop a grotesque, bulky body; no preoccupation with technique practice as in the jumps events. In fact, it might seem that all a distance runner needs to do to improve is simply run, run and run more.

In the past, middle-distance runners were often athletes who ran cross-country in the winter because they enjoyed running through different types of terrain. Some of them did not run track races in the summer because they found running laps around the track boring. Some used the track season to 'keep fit' in preparation for their cross-country racing season, whereas others were track athletes who used the cross-country season to 'keep fit' for the summer track season.

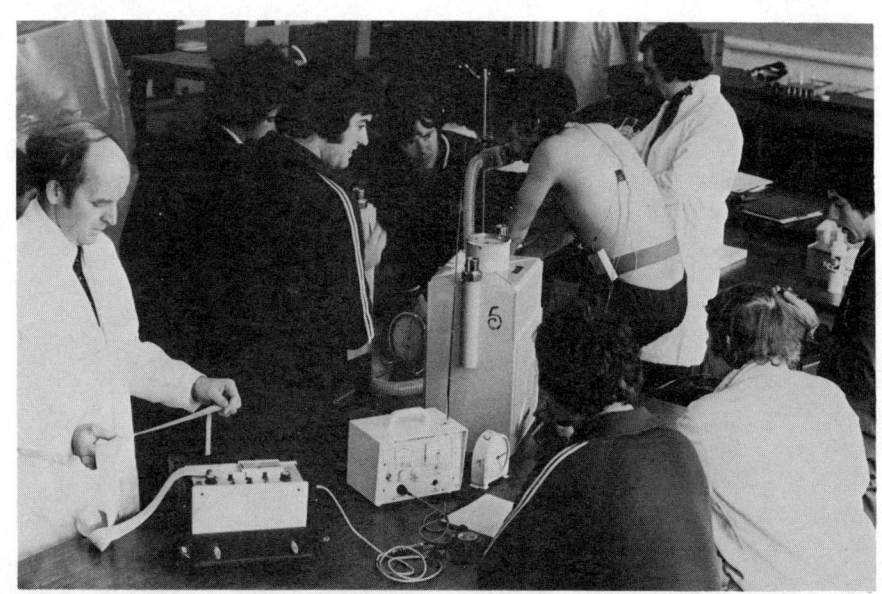

An international sportsman is seen here being subjected to a battery of tests in which a number of physiological measurements are taken to assist his coach in his schedule planning

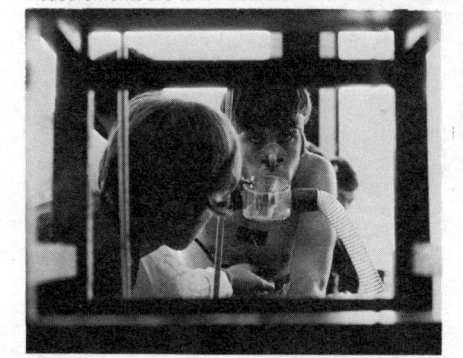

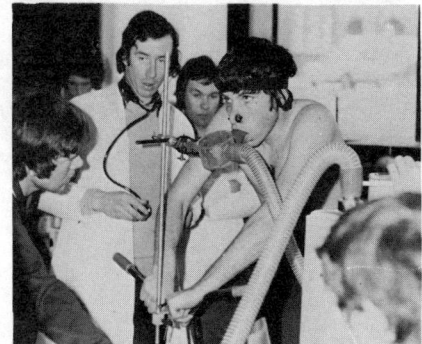

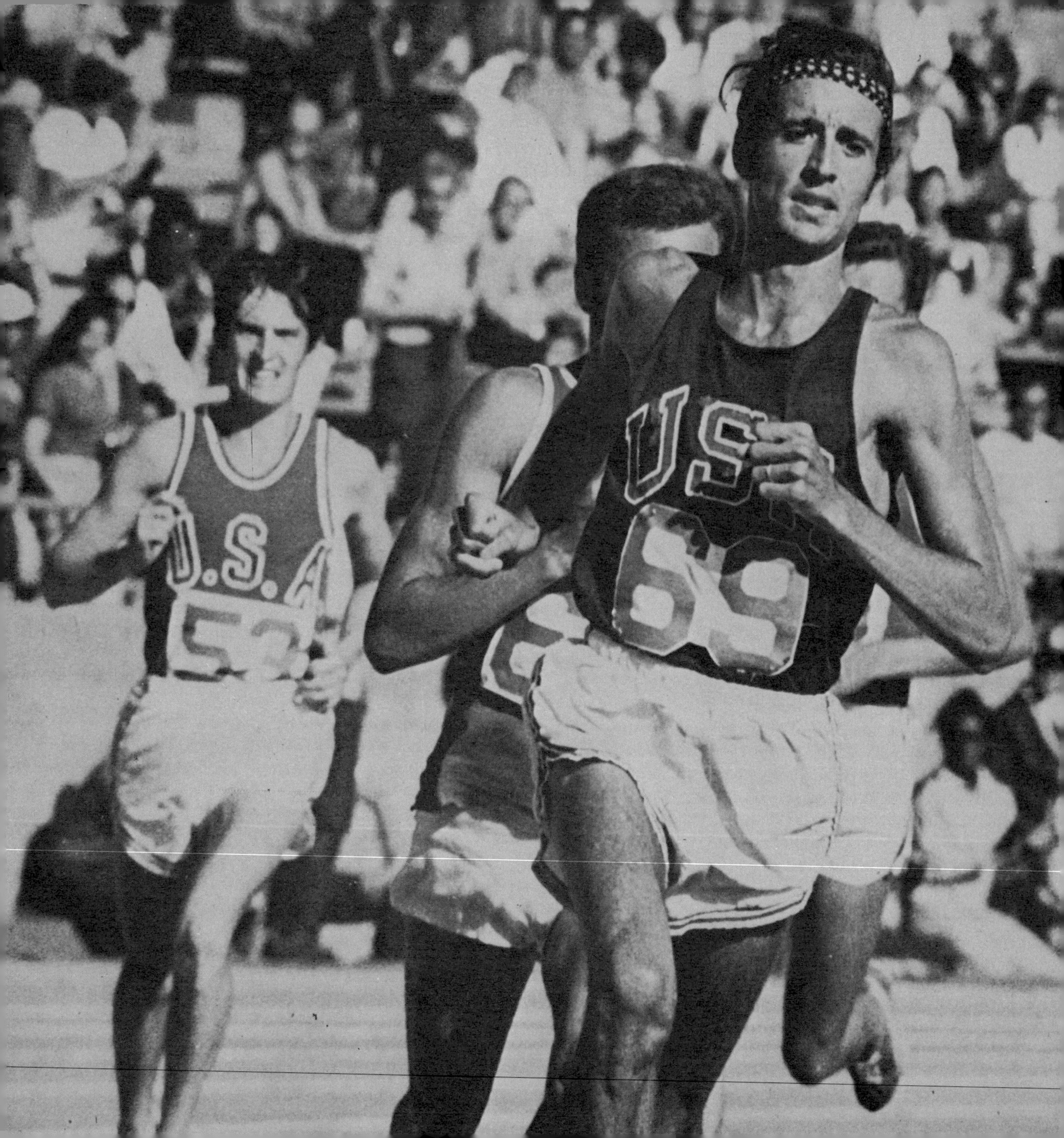
U.S.A
U.S
69

In women's events too, the somatotypes of the athletes differ

The variety of training appeals to the athletes

Sir Roger Bannister, Chris Chataway and Brain Hewson (all sub—4 minute mile runners) are examples of athletes who did not run competitively in the cross-country season. World track record holders Derek Ibbotson and Gordon Pirie, on the other hand, competed at international level in both cross-country and track events. We can see, therefore, that middle-distance runners are selective in the type of running they do. Similarly, a study of the types of training, the diets and the involvement of physiologists with middle-distance runners would indicate that nowadays, planning for improvement of the runners' abilities is more sophisticated than many people imagine.

The Athlete

World-class performers in middle and longer distance events have included a range of body types. There have been tall, slim athletes like Sir Roger Bannister, Kip Keino, Ron Clarke; diminutive, wiry athletes like Sydney Wooderson, Derek Johnson, Bruce Tulloh; muscular athletes such as Mike Rawson, Tom Courtney, Vladimir Knuts; and finally, a group of slightly disabled people, which includes asthmatics, and athletes with such deformities as a 'withered arm'.

The main fundamental to achieve success in running distances is the capacity to withstand hard work. This necessity for prolonged physical activity makes it vital that teachers and coaches should satisfy themselves that medical advice has been obtained and confirms that the athletes are physically capable of withstanding sustained physiological stress.

Additionally, the precaution should be taken of having regular checks made to ensure that when the intensity of training increases, or when the schoolchild is developing, no excessive amounts of work are being imposed.

Sound hearts, however, cannot be 'strained'. In fact, training makes the heart more efficient; running makes the athlete healthier. Another attractive feature of running is that for the less skilful person who does not achieve success at jumping or throwing, or who is not of the body type to be able to participate in games, this is an enjoyable, challenging outlet.

After much trial and error, athletes will find shoes that suit them

Even on cold days, clothing preferences differ. Some will wear gloves, and long sleeves; some will keep on lightweight track-suit bottoms; some wear the usual vest and shorts

Equipment

Though this may appear to be a superfluous section, there are a number of considerations for middle distance runners and cross-country runners:

- For track running, the athlete will eventually find a style of track shoe that suits him. A pair of shoes on which the spikes can be changed is recommended because of the many different types of surfaces that the athlete will be required to run on. With an all-weather track, shorter spikes will be required; on cinder tracks very long spikes will be used; on indoor tracks some athletes prefer to run barefoot or use a light training shoe.

Cross-country shoes are available in a number of forms. The sole can be ribbed or rubber studded to provide grip on slippery surfaces, whereas on a cross-country course that is flat, hard grass and dry, an athlete might choose to wear spiked shoes. Whatever is selected should be comfortable, previously worn (new shoes might cause blisters) and not too heavy.

- Athletes tend to wear the same vest repeatedly, because it is their 'lucky' vest, or their club vest. But there should be other considerations. If it is a very hot day, a string vest with many holes in it would physiologically be preferable to a cotton or nylon vest. On a cold, wintry day, light long-sleeved vests or shirts might be more appropriate. Vests, shorts and track suits should be washed regularly to prevent skin irritations.

- Useful adjuncts are a stop watch, ballet-tights and woollen hat for winter training, salt tablets for hot-weather climates, in which athletes tend to suffer from cramp, and a diary of training—recording not only what was done, but how it felt (this assists a coach in future schedule planning).

NAME	TIME	TIME DIFFERENCE FROM PREVIOUS RUNNER	TIME DIFFERENCE FROM LAST MAN
ANDREWS	10mins. 00secs.	0	1min. 50secs.
BLOGGS	10mins. 25secs.	25secs.	1min. 25secs.
CARTER	10mins. 40secs.	15secs.	1min. 10secs.
DAVIES	11mins. 00secs.	20secs.	50secs.
EVANS	11mins. 15secs.	15secs.	35secs.
FROST	11mins. 50secs.	35secs.	0

Progressive Stages

For the teacher or club coach who needs to build up school-children or athletes gradually to a point at which they can be given individual schedules, it is useful to get them involved enjoyably with groups of other people of the same age or ability. To begin with, the athlete will wish to know how he compares with others, so a short race over a cross-country course would be a useful guide. Dependent upon the ages of the athletes, a distance of perhaps approximately 3,000m could be selected. (British rules require that boys and girls must be at least thirteen years of age before they compete in cross-country races. For that age group the maximum distances are 5,000m for boys, and 3,000m for girls.)

1. Initial Races

The group set off all together from a point which ensures a sufficiently long distance to the first gate, gap in a hedge, or other funneling that could result in a bunching-up of athletes. On reaching the finish, each athlete is timed to the nearest second, and a ranking list is prepared showing the name of the athlete, his time and by what amount of time he beat the next man. An additional column shows in reverse order by how many minutes and/or seconds the last man was behind each runner, as illustrated above.

For the next occasion, the same race can be held, but this time each athlete will be motivated to attempt to
- win
- beat an athlete who beat him on the previous occasion
- beat his previous time
- narrow the time difference between himself and the runner ahead of him
- increase the distance between himself and the runner behind.

Such organisation creates interest and ensures that school-children and athletes put in more effort.

2. Ringing the Changes

Another form of running training that can be adopted is to take the final column of the race detailed above, and start a race with Frost setting off alone; his objective is not to be overtaken. 35 seconds later Evans sets off with the same objective and also attempts to overtake Frost. 50 seconds later Davies sets off and so on until, 1 min 50 secs after Frost started, Andrews leaves, hoping to beat his previous best time for the course and overtake as many athletes as possible en route.
The results of this race can show:
- who had the fastest time for the course
- which athletes beat their previous best time

- how many athletes overtook others during the race, etc.

Such changes of runs lend interest, provide incentive for greater effort, and often increase the enjoyment. Further modes of training in the early stages can include pairing off the runners, e.g. Andrews and Frost (the best and poorest), Bloggs and Evans, Carter and Davies. The objective of such a race would be that the combined times of each pair would be recorded, and those obtaining the lowest time would win.

3. Hares and Hounds and Paper Chase

Other popular forms of running have included in the past Hares and Hounds, where one or two athletes set off over a known course a minute or so before the remainder who attempt to catch him/them before he/they return(s) back to the starting place. In countries where the litter laws permit it, an interesting form of competition is for two runners to set off with bags of small pieces of paper (or sawdust, or chalk) on their backs. Their course is a secret, and they are given one or two minutes' start. The pursuers see the direction in which the athletes have gone, but once out of sight, they can change direction provided they leave a trail of chalk, paper, etc., showing where they have gone. The objective is to catch the trail-leavers before they return back to the starting point.

Related to this type of activity is orienteering, a sport which involves participants with maps and compasses covering a predetermined route, visiting a number of checkpoints, and attempting to complete the course as quickly as they can. For further details see *EP Sport Orienteering* (EP Publishing Ltd., 1976).

4. Track Practices

Having provided a base of fitness through increasing amounts of enjoyable running, the teacher or coach can begin to organise other practices based at the track. In the first instance, athletes can be required to carry out simple repetition runs similar to those outlined in the 'Sprinting' chapter of this book; then can follow an introduction to the *paarlauf* (pair-running) system. Paarlauf is an interesting form of training or racing in which a racing distance, say eight laps of the track, is first decided upon. The athletes are divided into pairs and each pair decides how to divide the race between them; only one of the athletes needs to be running at any one time. There are a number of ways of doing it:

(i) Athlete 'A' can run the first four laps and Athlete 'B' the last four;

(ii) Athlete 'A' can run the first two

laps, then Athlete 'B' two laps, then Athlete 'A' two laps, concluding with Athlete 'B' two laps;
(iii) They can run alternate laps;
(iv) Athlete 'A' can run 200m and touch Athlete 'B' (as in a relay), who runs the next 200m. In the meantime Athlete 'A' cuts across the centre grass area of the track to his original starting point where Athlete 'B' hands over the race to him. Athlete 'B' also cuts across the track ready to take over at his own 200m point.
(v) If 'A' is a better athlete than 'B' it may be decided to allocate over half of the running to 'A'.

Having begun to mix track work with cross-country practices, the teacher or coach will now be able to observe which athletes are ready to be given individual training programmes.

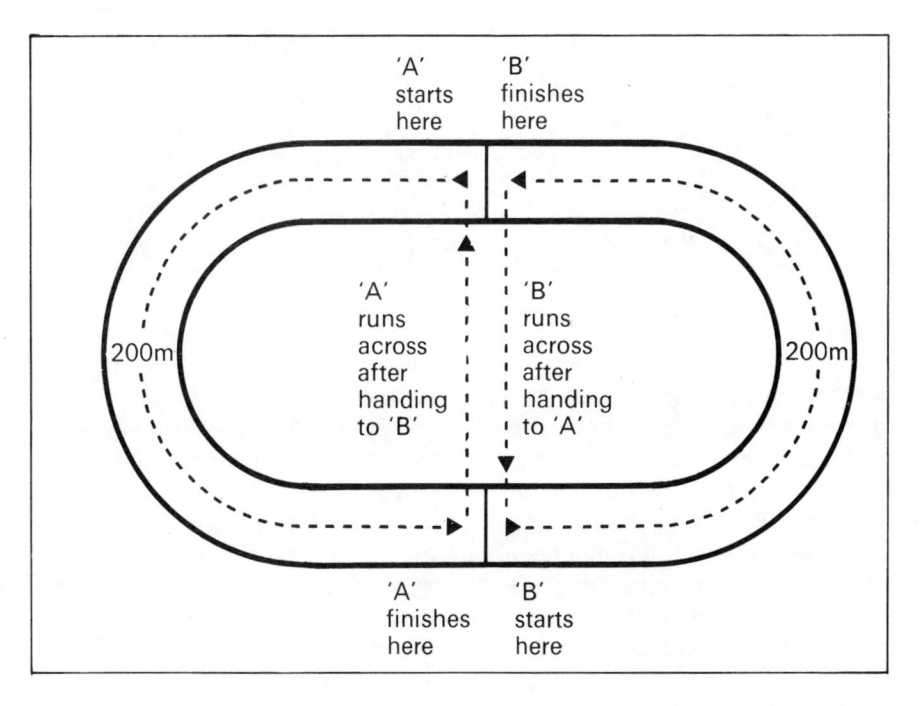

Training—Theories

Some athletes tend to adopt track running styles in cross-country races. Sometimes this is inappropriate and results in wasted expenditure of energy

Style

Obviously an uneconomical technique of running must be cured by the teacher or coach, but it is stressed that there is no ideal method of running. Emil Zatopek adopted a head and shoulder roll with tongue hanging out and an agonised facial expression; Arthur Wint had a massive stride length and a most relaxed look about him; Bruce Tulloh shuffled along in bare feet with arms bunched tightly across his body.

The important criterion is comfort. If an athlete's natural style is mechanically inefficient, causing him to expend extra energy, then the coach will modify the style; otherwise, there need be no interference. Breathing should be through the mouth and nose, there should be no attempt to lengthen the stride, and there should be a minimum of tension especially in the face and neck muscles.

Towards the end of a race (and, in the case of cross-country running, when running uphill), the style will necessarily change, the knees coming through higher and the arms driving more. In fact, a sprinter's style will be adopted.

Long-distance as Training

It is not only athletes of the distant past who have used the long distance method for the bulk of their training. Peter Snell and Murry Halberg of New Zealand were both Olympic medallists trained by Arthur Lydiard, who claimed that all his runners were *marathon* runners. That is, though Snell won the gold medal in the 1960 Olympics in the 800 metres, Lydiard expected him to run marathon distances in training. Some athletes who believe in the value of this system will train well over 100 miles in total each week, and will include runs of 20 miles or more on at least one day. Some athletes doing this kind of training are 800 metres runners! But athletes should not rely solely on this method, for though it has an advantageous effect on the circulo-respiratory system and therefore provides a good basis for other types of training, actual racing consists of changes of pace including fast bursts as well as the slower pace, and so the heart needs to be accustomed to a variety of changes during training.

Interval Training

Another group of athletes of yesteryear and the present day have preferred this systematic form of training, including Paavo Nurmi, Gordon Pirie, Vladimir Kuts, Emil Zatopek and Sir Roger Bannister.

In interval training, the objective is to adapt the heart to the stress of running in endurance events. When training over distances in the region of 100, 200 and 400m, it has been found that middle-distance runners' hearts become stronger and pump blood around the muscles in greater volume, provided they run the chosen distance fast and take a pause of about 45–90 seconds before they run the next repetition.

German physiologists have shown that after a fast run of 200m the heart fills rapidly with blood. If the athlete jogs slowly for about 45 seconds, the amount of blood arriving at the heart is decreased. Should the athlete then repeat the procedure many times, with 'intervals' of sprinting followed by 'intervals' of slow jogging, the cavities of the heart increase in size and adapt themselves to receive more blood, thus providing more fresh blood to be supplied throughout the body. During a training session, this system can gradually lose its effect. This has been shown to occur when an athlete's heart rate is over 180 beats per minute. Coaches therefore tend to limit their athletes' sprints to the period when the heart-rate is between 120 and 150 beats per minute, the rest between each run allowing the heart-rate to drop to that range.

Criticisms of the method include:
(a) it is boring
(b) it makes an athlete too dependent on stop-watch performance
(c) the volume of blood pumped out of the heart at each stroke is only one consideration, the number of strokes per minute also being important.

Tempo Running

In addition to efficient hearts and lungs, athletes must also consider the fatigue in the arms, shoulders and leg muscles that is evident at the end of a race. One form of training that prepares athletes for this is where the coach requires them to do very fast runs between which there is a very short rest. Thus the athlete is expected to perform with great amounts of lactic acid in the muscle incurring what is known as 'oxygen debt'. Eventually the athlete manages to cope with this anaerobic activity and the pain of the fatigue.

This is an arduous form of training even for experienced athletes and should not constitute the sole method of training.

Occasional runs of men and women athletes provide an enjoyable change. The women are extended by having to keep up with the men. When the women have finished their part of the run, of course, the men will continue training for a longer period of time ▶

◀ A part of an interesting 'Fartlek' course

◀ A slippery, muddy slope is as hard to run up as sand-dunes

Fartlek

This Scandinavian form of training is literally 'speed-play'. It places the onus on the athlete to decide when to place the effort and is best carried out over a country course which provides an interesting array of hills, fast stretches and rough ground. Though an experienced athlete will be able to 'push' himself to include more fast running stretches than slower ones, less experienced athletes might need direction. A coach or teacher could accompany his athletes, giving directions such as, 'we will begin by jogging 800 metres'; 'now sprint 100 metres'; 'now jog 200 metres'; 'now walk down this hill'; 'now run as fast as possible to the end of this path'; 'now walk 200 metres'; 'now as fast as possible to the top of this hill'.

Resistance Running

Arthur Lydiard in New Zealand, Percy Cerutty in Australia, Gundar Haegg in Sweden and Jim Alford in Wales all had something in common—the insistence on frequent hill-running as part of their athletes' training. Whether the hills are mud, snow, sand or coal seems not to matter provided athletes are required to run up them fast, using their arms vigorously, and repeat the runs often.

Other forms of resistance running include harness-running, described on p. 29, running in heavy boots, running with sacks of sand on the back and running with weighted belts. Whenever a coach employs these methods he should consider the objective, and whether the same effect could be obtained in another way. Sometimes coaches tend to become slaves to one method which has value only at limited periods during a year.

Weights and Circuits

Weight training and circuit training are valuable forms of work for middle-distance runners and are fully described in *Conditioning for Sport* by this author (EP Publishing, 1975).

Training—Schedules

Devising schedules for middle-distance and cross-country runners is no easy task—they differ so much in capacity for work, physiological make-up, conscientiousness and occupation! An enthusiastic office-boy who has little talent will need different treatment from a farm labourer of similar age who has great potential but whose job leaves him less than willing to cover great distances on the track at the end of a day.

All that can be provided here are mere guide-lines, and intelligent teachers and coaches will adapt them to suit the ages, abilities, sex and disposition of their own athletes. It will be noticed that in some cases two sessions per day are noted; these are for better athletes. In fact, some internationals train three times per day with a long run before breakfast, a session at lunch-time and a further session in the evening. They have spent a number of years building up to this, so one good session should suffice for beginners.

The important thing to remember is that variety is a pre-requisite to improvement.

800 metres MEN (Off-season)
(Good Standard Athlete)

	DAY 1	20 miles road run
	DAY 2	Run 800m on grass four times with a 3-minute interval between each run
	DAY 3	5 miles sustained run Weight training for arms and shoulders
	DAY 4	Run 400m on the track in about 62 seconds Repeat eleven times, with a 2-minute recovery interval between each run
	DAY 5	Fartlek for 45 minutes Harness running
	DAY 6	6 miles 'easy run'
	DAY 7	Competition (cross-country) or Hard 45-minute Fartlek and weight training session

800 metres MEN (During season)
(Good Standard Athlete)

	DAY 1	30-minute Fartlek
	DAY 2	Run 400m in under 58 seconds; repeat seven times Run 200m in under 28 seconds; repeat once Sprint 100m, fast; repeat once
	DAY 3	Jog for 3 miles Run 1200m at an even pace in about 3 minutes 15 seconds; repeat once Run 300m time trial
	DAY 4	Run 600m in under 85 seconds Run 200m in under 26 seconds; repeat twice Sprint 100m in under 13 seconds; repeat five times
	DAY 5	Run 200m ten times Run 400m twice Throughout these runs practise pace judgement, bearing the next competition in mind
	DAY 6	Carry out usual pre-race-day routine. Some may rest, others do a steady jog over a short distance
	DAY 7	Competition (400m, 800m or 1500m)

800 metres WOMEN (Off-season)
(Good Standard Athlete)

	DAY 1	8 miles road run
	DAY 2	Run 800m on grass four times, with a 4-minute interval between each run
	DAY 3	3 miles sustained run Weight-training for arms and shoulders
	DAY 4	Run 400m on the track in 78 seconds Repeat seven times with a 3-minute interval between each run
	DAY 5	Fartlek for 30 minutes Possibly some circuit-training
	DAY 6	4 miles 'easy run'
	DAY 7	Competition (cross-country) or 30-minute Fartlek, or harness running

800 metres WOMEN (During season)
(Good Standard Athlete)

	DAY 1	20-minute Fartlek
	DAY 2	Run 400m in under 72 seconds; repeat four times Run 200m in under 35 seconds; repeat once Sprint 100m, fast; repeat once
	DAY 3	Jog for 3000m Run 1000m, evenly paced; repeat once Run 300m time trial
	DAY 4	Run 600m in under 105 seconds Run 200m in under 34 seconds; repeat twice Sprint 100m, fast; repeat three times
	DAY 5	Run 200m six times Run 400m twice Throughout these runs practise pace judgement, bearing the next competition in mind
	DAY 6	Carry out normal pre-race-day routine. Some athletes rest completely, others jog a short distance
	DAY 7	Competition (400m, 800m, or 1500m)

1500 metres MEN (Off-season)
(Good Standard Athlete)

DAY 1		20 miles road run
DAY 2		Run 1600m on grass four times, with a 5-minute interval between each run
DAY 3		Hard 10,000m sustained run Weight training or circuit training
DAY 4		Run 400m in approximately 62/63 seconds; repeat fifteen times, with $1\frac{1}{2} - 2$ minutes recovery interval between each run
DAY 5		50 minutes Fartlek or hill running
DAY 6		8 miles 'easy' run
DAY 7		Competition (cross-country) or Hard Fartlek, up to 1 hour

1500 metres MEN (During season)
(Good Standard Athlete)

DAY 1	1-hour Fartlek
DAY 2	Run 2400m time trial Jog 2400m Cover 100m using fast strides; repeat three times
DAY 3	Jog 4 miles Run 1200m twice, with an even pace Run 400m fast
DAY 4	Sprint 200m in under 26 seconds; repeat three times Sprint 100m in under 13 seconds; repeat three times Sprint 400m in under 56 seconds; repeat once
DAY 5	Jog 2 miles Run 600m four times; practise pace judgement, bearing the next competition in mind
DAY 6	Carry out normal pre-race-day routine
DAY 7	Competition (800m, 1500m, or 5,000m)

1500 metres WOMEN (Off-season)
(Good Standard Athlete)

DAY 1	Up to 10 miles road run
DAY 2	Run 1600 m on grass four times, with approximately 7 minutes interval between each run
DAY 3	Hard 5,000m sustained run Circuit training
DAY 4	Run 400m in under approximately 80 seconds, with a 3-minute interval between each run
DAY 5	40 minutes Fartlek or hill runs
DAY 6	6 miles 'easy' run
DAY 7	Competition (cross-country) or Hard Fartlek, up to 45 minutes

1500 metres WOMEN (During season)
(Good Standard Athlete)

DAY 1	30-minute Fartlek
DAY 2	Run 2000m time trial Jog 2000m Sprint 100m, fast, three times
DAY 3	Jog 3000m Run 1200m at an even pace; repeat once Run 400m fast
DAY 4	Run 200m in under 34 seconds; repeat twice Sprint 100m fast; repeat twice Run 400m in under 70 seconds; repeat once
DAY 5	Jog 2000m Run 600m three times; practise pace judgement, bearing the next competition in mind
DAY 6	Carry out usual pre-race-day routine
DAY 7	Competition (800m or 1500m)

Cross-country and 5,000 metres runners (MEN)
(Off-season)

DAY 1	20 miles road run
DAY 2	1-hour Fartlek Weight training or circuit training
DAY 3	Interval or Tempo-training, e.g.: Run 1000m once; run 800m twice; run 600m three times; run 400m four times
DAY 4	10-mile run (including hills, or possibly some resistance work or weight training)
DAY 5	Run 5 miles on grass
DAY 6	Carry out usual pre-race-day routine, or run for 30 minutes with a mixture of fast and slow running
DAY 7	Competition, or time trial, or Fartlek, or harness running, etc.

Cross-country and 5,000 metres runners (MEN)
(During season)

DAY 1	1 – 2 hours Fartlek
DAY 2	Run 400m in under 62 seconds; repeat eleven times, with 1½ minutes recovery interval between each run Jog for 15 minutes Run 800m four times
DAY 3	6 miles hard sustained run
DAY 4	Run 1200m at 5000m racing speed twice, with 10 minutes jogging between runs Run 600m eight times
DAY 5	Stride quickly over distances of 200m for 10 minutes Jog for 10 minutes Run 400m fast; repeat five times Run 200m fast; repeat five times
DAY 6	Carry out usual pre-race-day routine
DAY 7	Competition (1500 – 10,000 metres)

Rules

The usual track rules apply and in particular, middle-distance runners should comply with the following:

(a) Refreshments are not to be provided in races of 10 miles or less.
(b) Competitors taking drugs will be liable to disqualification.
(c) Competitors must at once retire from a race if ordered to do so by a member of the official medical staff.
(d) Numbers must be worn on the chest.
(e) Clothing must be made of a material which is not transparent when wet.
(f) No person other than the official time-keepers shall indicate 'lap times' to athletes.
(g) Starting blocks are *not* permitted in races of 800 metres and over.
(h) Any competitor who jostles, runs across or obstructs another athlete so that his progress is affected shall be liable to disqualification.
(i) Athletes who voluntarily leave the track or course shall not be allowed to continue in the race.

Athletes no's 38 and 24 are 'legal'. The athlete on the extreme right will be disqualified for having no number. The athlete third from right will be disqualified for removing his vest during a race

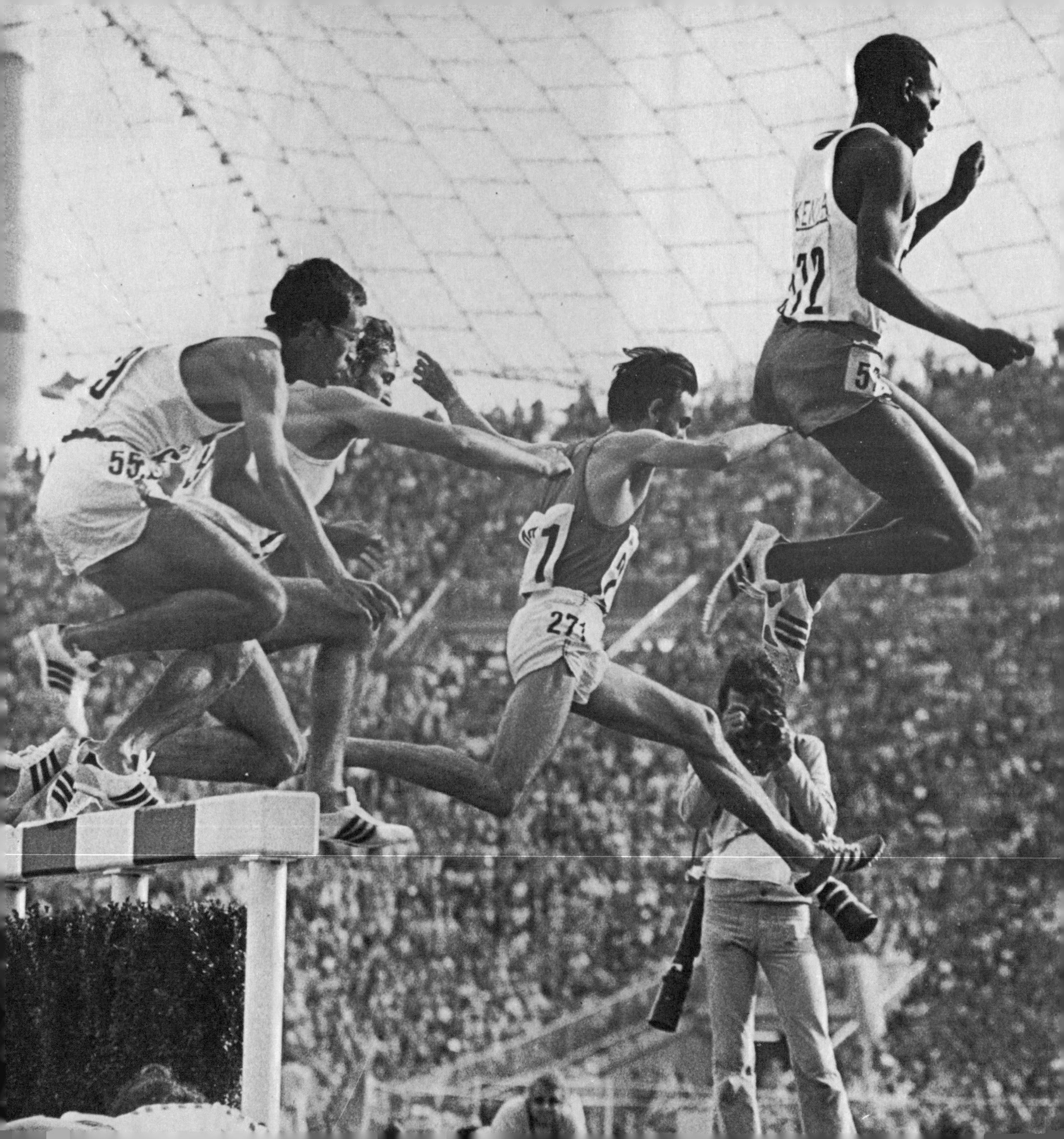

Steeplechase

The steeplechase event in the Olympic Games is a 3,000 metres race on the track during which the athlete has to clear hurdles twenty-eight times and a water jump seven times. It is therefore a most arduous race demanding endurance, skill, courage and tactical planning.

The Athlete

Past steeplechasers have been either cross-country runners who use this as their summer event 'to keep fit', or runners who have been converted from middle-distances. Nowadays, steeplechase specialists have emerged and those who arrive via one of the above-mentioned routes soon discover that it is not an easy event, and that the standards at top-class level are very high.

Steeplechasing has also appeared in schools in recent years, though boys run either 2,000 or 1,500m, dependent upon their age. It is not a recognised women's event, neither is it recommended for them.

No particular body type succeeds in steeplechase, but it is a tough event needing the middle-distance runner's endurance and determination, and the hurdler's skill and versatility.

Equipment

- No personal equipment additional to the requirements of a middle-distance runner is required, except that the rule regarding the forbidding of transparent shorts relates particularly to steeplechasers, who tend to get wet during the race!
- The steeplechase hurdles are different from the usual track race hurdles. Steeplechase hurdles are of solid construction because athletes do not have to hurdle them; if they wish they may step onto them. They are 91·4cm high and 3·66m wide.

The water jump is 3·66m long and the same width. The water is 70cm deep, tapering off the level of the track at the end away from the hurdle.

The track can have the water jump placed in a number of positions, as illustrated.

USUAL LAYOUT

Measurements are as follows:

Start to beginning of first full lap (No jumping or hurdling)	242m
From beginning of first full lap to 1st hurdle	15.80m
1st hurdle to 2nd hurdle	79m
2nd hurdle to 3rd hurdle	79m
3rd hurdle to water jump	79m
Water Jump to 4th hurdle	62.20m
4th hurdle to finish line	79m

7 full laps are run, making total distance 3,000m

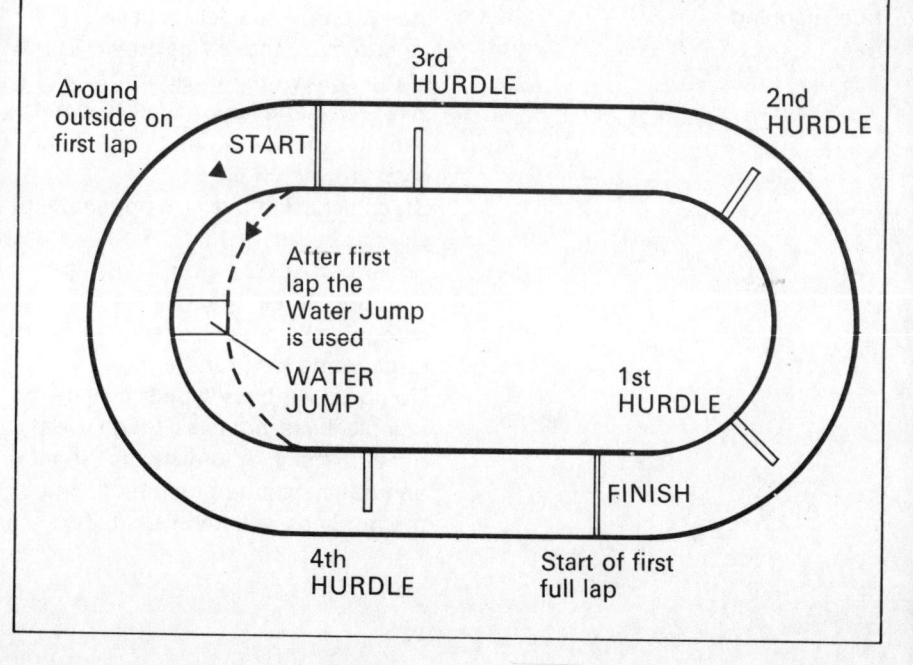

Around outside on first lap

START

3rd HURDLE

2nd HURDLE

After first lap the Water Jump is used

WATER JUMP

1st HURDLE

FINISH

4th HURDLE

Start of first full lap

ALTERNATIVE LAYOUTS:

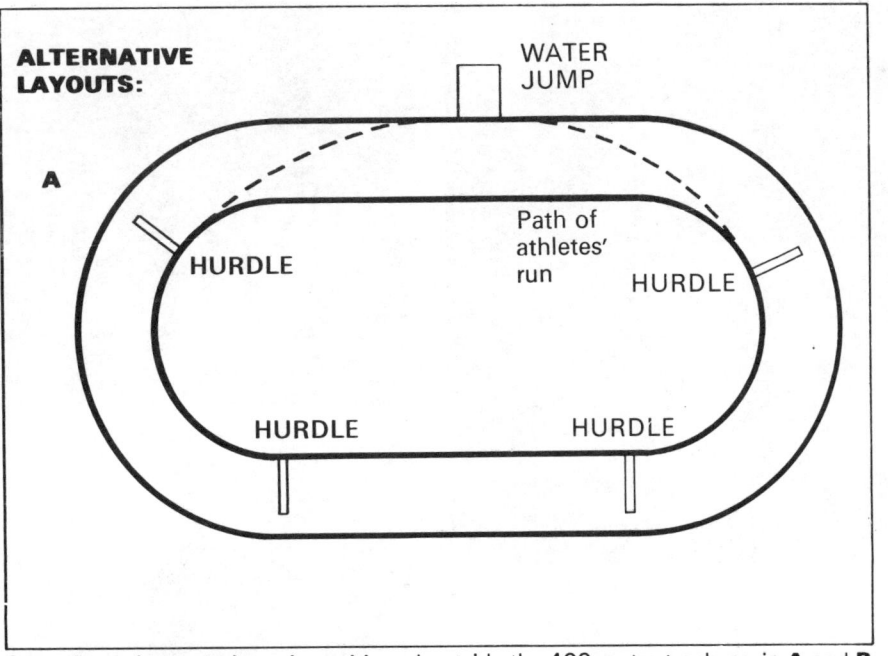

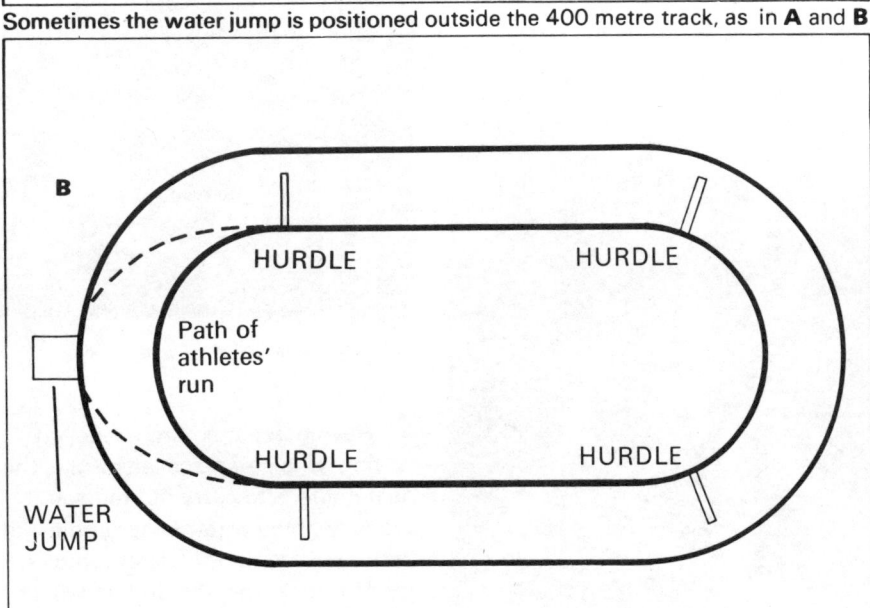

A — WATER JUMP, HURDLE, Path of athletes' run, HURDLE, HURDLE, HURDLE

Sometimes the water jump is positioned outside the 400 metre track, as in **A** and **B**

B — HURDLE, HURDLE, Path of athletes' run, HURDLE, HURDLE, WATER JUMP

Progressive Stages

1. First, the intending steeplechaser needs to be soundly fit, and have had his endurance developed over a long period of time by the practices described in the chapter on middle-distance and cross-country running.

2. Secondly, the intending steeplechaser needs to have developed a good hurdling technique over a 3ft (1m) high barrier. This will have been acquired over a period of time in practices described in the chapter on hurdles.

3. Additional practice must be given for the water jump technique. This will be done first of all by getting the athlete to run, step on a steeplechase hurdle, and continue running a short distance. Effort will be applied on top of the hurdle so that the athlete will be driving forward as far away from the hurdle as possible.

Practising the step on to the hurdle

This athlete keeps his centre of gravity low as he steps on to the water jump hurdle

Practising the drive off the hurdle

Driving for the far end of the water jump

4. Having acquired proficiency at driving off a steeplechase hurdle, the next stage is to carry out the same practice at the water jump hurdle, but with no water in the water jump; at the learner stage, the athlete will not be driving sufficiently far off the hurdle.

Left: better steeplechasers save time and energy by *hurdling* over the hurdles (left)—but not over the water jump!

Others, like the athlete below, jump over every obstacle, wasting much time and energy

Training

During the winter, steeplechasers will train with a mixture of cross-country racing, middle-distance running, and occasional hurdling.
During the summer, steeplechasers will continue a middle-distance runner's programme, adding hurdling and water jump techniques on one or two days, dependent upon the runner's level of skill.

Rules

(a) Every competitor must go over or through the water at the water jump.
(b) Every competitor must go over every hurdle by hurdling, jumping or vaulting over them. He may place a foot on each hurdle.
(c) The usual rules for middle-distance events also apply.

5. The final beginner stage is the use of a check-mark a short distance before the water jump, so that the athlete can arrange his feet in such a way that he can be running fast at the water jump hurdle.
Then comes the point at which the athlete must be able to run laps, in each of which four hurdles and a water jump are included

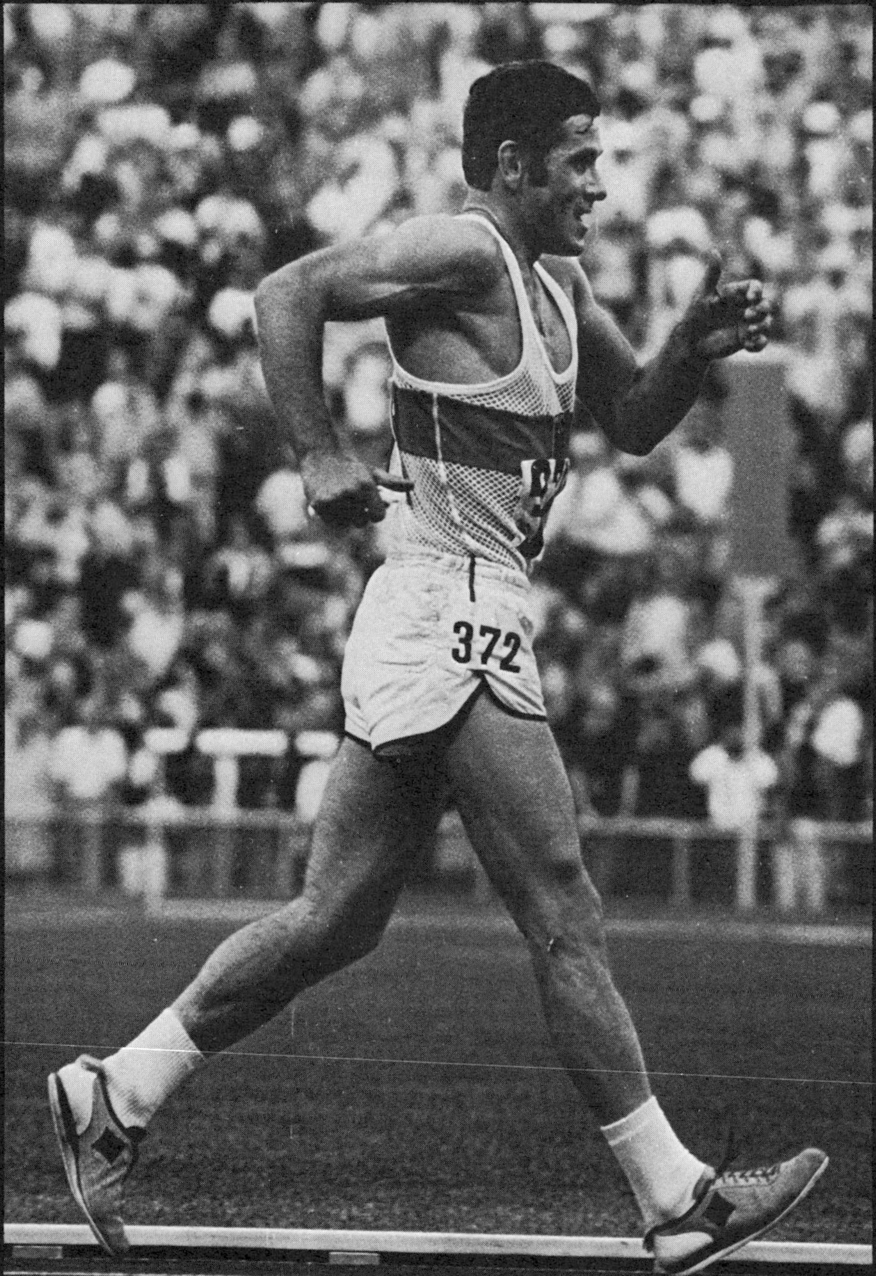
372

Walking Races

This illustrates a very good 'legal' walking style. The back toe does not break contact with the ground until the front heel touches

Here the walker demonstrates an 'illegal' style, and would be disqualified. His rear foot is off the floor before the front foot is grounded

'Walking is progression by steps so taken that unbroken contact with the ground is maintained. At each step, the advancing foot of the walker must make contact with the ground before the rear foot leaves the ground.' (A.A.A. Rule 108)

Many people regard walking competitions as 'artificial' events; they would contend that if someone wished to get from A to B in a hurry, he would run. Many also regard walking races as a hilarious form of activity to observe, for the strange style of hip-wiggling and arm action tends to bring mirth to the faces of those who know little about race-walking.

Race-walkers defend their sport with a number of points. Firstly, they would point to the 'artificiality' of pole-vaulting, hammer-throwing and even the crouch start in sprinting. They would claim that in fact walking is a very natural activity, and that the style racers adopt is merely the result of man applying his brain to the task of making walking more efficient within the rules laid down. Secondly, they would emphasise the health aspect of walking, and the fact that it can be cheap with no special equipment or clothing needed. Thirdly, they would point out that Olympic competition is available for walkers, whereas it is not, for instance, for caber-tossing, and so walkers have world records and championships for which to strive. Finally, walkers would remind their critics that their sport can be continued throughout life, over different terrain, by men and women and children. In fact they would stress that throughout the world, the best walkers tend to be well into their thirties, thus making the Olympic Games a balance between younger competitors (e.g. in swimming) and older competitors.

What about the unbiased teacher or coach who is considering whether or not he or she should introduce race walking as an additional event in the school or club? There seem to be a number of considerations. Are there opportunities for competition locally, or not too far away? If the only competition is likely to be against one's fellow athletes or pupils, boredom may well set in, whereas if competition against other clubs or schools can easily be organised, there is an incentive for training. Another consideration is judging. If there are no qualified judges, or people who can interpret the rules intelligently, then race-walking for beginners can become a disguised run, and a tendency to cheat can creep in. Furthermore, if the club or school has a wide range of events and sports that seem to cater for all of the people, then it may well be that the time to introduce race-walking has not arrived.

But if a group of children or athletes shows interest in walking, and if they are not achieving success in other events, teachers and coaches should seriously consider introducing walking, and then secure the necessary judges and competitions to satisfy an established need.

The Athlete

No particular body types succeed more than others in race-walking, that is if it is taken for granted that the obese and the very weak are unlikely to be successful. International 'stars' have included Olympic gold medallist Don Thompson, a very small, light-framed individual who wore spectacles, and who in his normal clothes would not have impressed any onlooker as being the layman's idea of a world-class athlete. Another Olympic gold medal winner, Ken Matthews, was very tall and muscular and could have been mistaken for a top-class high jumper or hurdler. One generalisation about race-walkers can be made, however. They must build up their strength and endurance with walking, running, exercises and weights, because race-walking is a very demanding activity that puts a strain on all muscle groups. In view of the fact that walking races tend to be over longer distances,

This particular athlete prefers to wear his vest outside his shorts to allow fresh air to reach his midriff. He also dispenses with socks in races up to 10,000 metres. For races above that distance, and in dusty conditions, he finds value in using socks. Athletes differ in preference

athletes should be well-prepared over a period of time before they are entered for competitions.

Walkers tend to suffer from leg problems such as 'shin splints', that is pain in the front of the legs. These are often due to weakness and can be overcome gradually as the athlete grows stronger. During a race, the pain can only be relieved by slowing down, and similarly in training it is better not to stop altogether, but to 'walk out' the pain. Another problem that arises is at the knee joint, onto which the bodyweight is forced in the normal walking style. Some athletes are unable to lock the knee during the walk due to weakness. As the strength increases, and exercises stretch the ligaments, the knee problems tend to disappear.

Surprising as it may seem, some walkers also suffer from abdominal pains. This is often due to weakness in the stomach muscles and in time the pain lessens. Sometimes, however, the pain is the result of a bad trunk position, and the style needs attention. In addition, the usual breathing difficulties such as 'stitch' appear in walking. A good warm-up before the race, no heavy meals before the race, and an improvement in fitness will tend to alleviate breathing problems. To summarise, one could say that like all athletics events, race-walking needs careful preparation, hard training, good food, helpful coaching and dedication. There is a great deal of skill required, but not of the nature of the flexible pole-vaulting skill, for instance. Race-walking can suit a large number of people who would not otherwise take part in athletics, but it is not an easy event, to be taken lightly, and teachers, coaches, athletes and schoolchildren should ensure that race-walking receives the adequate preparation which would be given to any other athletics event.

Equipment

- At an early stage, strong shoes, training shoes or strong plimsolls are adequate. Blisters tend to be a problem for walkers; in time, the athlete will be able to discern which shoes and socks and foot powders suit him best, and he will ensure that new footwear is well 'broken in' before being used in competition.
- For winter training, track suits or warm clothes will be necessary to protect muscles from injury. During cold weather competition, long sleeves and gloves can be an asset, whereas in very hot climates, 'aertex' vests will be worn. To summarise, it is sufficient to say that a minimum of clothing and equipment is necessary for race-walking, and athletes will soon select those items that give greatest comfort and efficiency.

Race Walking Techniques

At the beginning, children or athletes will be under the impression that walking is easy. Within minutes, it will become apparent that walking in races requires about a one-third increase in stride length, a considerable increase in hip-rotation, a very vigorous arm action and a changed foot/leg angle. All of this convinces the beginner that an analysis is necessary to ensure greater efficiency which will also make the race-walking less of an effort.

Because we tend to think mainly of the legs as the propulsive force in race-walking, the leg action will be considered first.

Leg Action

The race-walking rules require that the knee of the leading leg is straight when it reaches the vertical position, and that the heel of the leading leg touches the ground before the rear foot leaves the ground. Therefore a good technique must be developed in the early stages, not only to ensure no waste of effort, but also to ensure that a legal style is learned.

Beginners tend to find the legal style a strain, particularly at the knees, and they tend to slap the front foot down. In fact the heel of the leading leg should reach the ground first with the knee practically straight, but with the thigh muscles relaxed. As soon as contact with the ground is made, the muscles tighten and a **pulling** action begins which straightens the leg.

During this time, the rear leg remains straight as long as possible to keep the body going at speed. Thus we have a **pulling** effect from the front leg and a **pushing** effect from the rear leg. But this effective propulsion depends on correct foot action. The rear foot must not leave the ground until the drive is continued right up to the point of the

Here the walker demonstrates excellent arm drive, relaxation and stride length

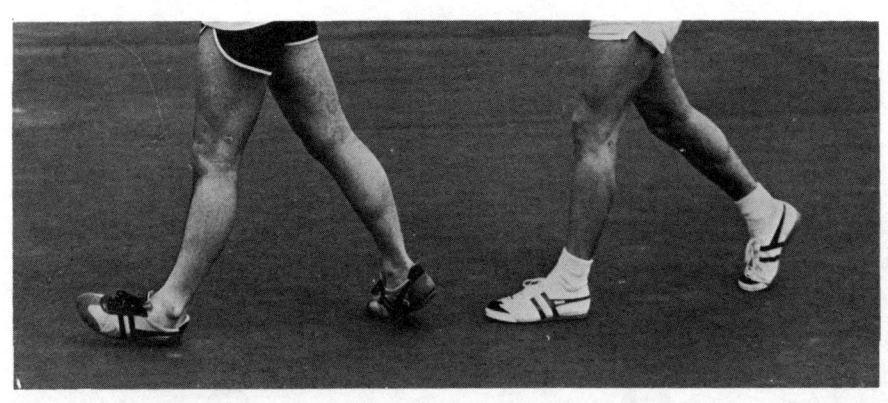

Two walking styles to be encountered. The front walker demonstrates that the heel always touches first, and the second walker illustrates a beginner's tendency to place the front foot down flat

toe. Beginners raise their rear leg when the ball of the foot is on the ground, thus losing almost 8 centimetres of stride length. As the aim is to obtain a stride length of about 1.2 metres (for adults), and as the good walkers take about three strides every second, the rear foot must drive right up onto the toe.

The front heel will land first and a smooth transition is made onto the ball of the foot, with a drive off the inside ball of the foot area, finishing off with the toe. Some tend to use a splay-foot style to gain extra distance; this is permissible provided that the swinging-through action concentrates on a toe-pointing-forward movement, and not a wasteful rotated foot action.

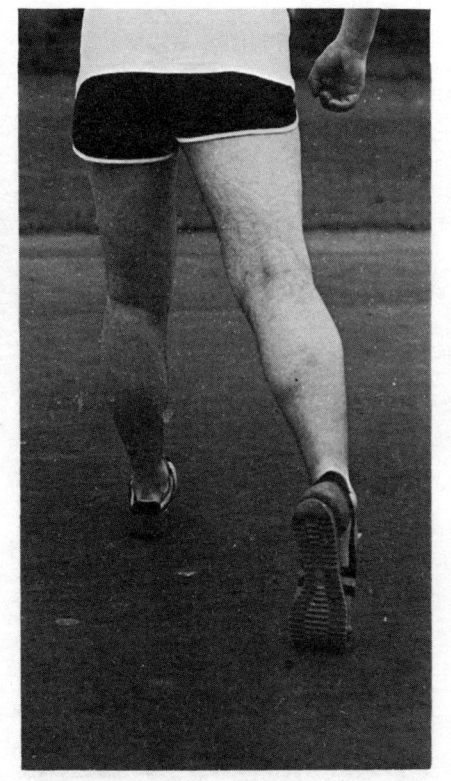

A rear view of a good walking style in which the athlete drives up onto the back toe while making contact first with the heel in front

Hip Action

When the speed of normal walking increases, one tends to rotate the hips so that the stride length and speed increase. Additionally there is a lowering of the body as illustrated. In race-walking, the hips swing forward and also one side is elevated higher than the other. This is automatic and needs no undue emphasis in coaching. The gain in stride length from this hip movement can be as much as 20 centimetres. The eliminating of the body raising and lowering is an energy conserver.

An illustration of a tendency of the rear foot to twist slightly so that the push comes occasionally from the inside of the ball of the walker's foot

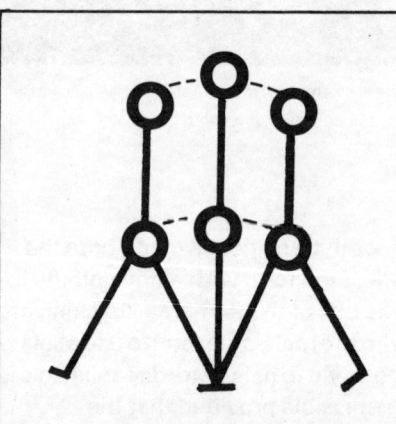

Normal walking action, hips kept facing forward.

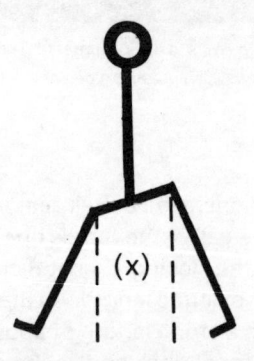

Race-walking action, hips rotating and extra stride length indicated (x).

Right: the first man is able to maintain a relaxed style whereas those following demonstrate an energy-sapping, tense style

Below: the race is nearing its end. The two front walkers are unnecessarily 'getting their heads down', which will in fact reduce their stride length and slow them down. The two rear walkers are looking well ahead, but are too stiff and jerky in their style to overtake relaxed walkers.

Head and Trunk Positions

Holding the head too far forward creates extra muscle tension and cuts down the rotation of the hips, thus shortening the stride length. Holding the head too far back causes extra effort, uses up energy wastefully and shortens the stride. As in running events, the ideal head position is in natural alignment with the body, with the eyes gazing forwards down the track (not immediately in front of the feet, and not up into the sky).

The best trunk position is a vertical one. Any undue tendency to lean forward or back will adversely affect the performance. There are occasions, however, when there is a need to make adjustments to the head and trunk. When walking up hills a *slight* lean forward will be necessary; this will facilitate the hip action. Downhill walking needs particular attention to avoid disqualification; a *slight* lean backwards will assist in slowing down the speed of the walk which otherwise might become a run.

A very good arm action. The front arm drives across the body at about 90° at the elbow, the fingers relaxed. The rear arm is driving hard backwards

A side view of an excellent arm action. The rear upper arm is almost horizontal, there is over 90° at the elbow, the fingers are relaxed. The front arm is reaching forward slightly and is well across the body

Arm Action

As in running events, the arm action is of considerably more importance than people generally believe. The race-walking arm style should be with an emphasis on relaxation at the shoulders but bent at the elbow. The arm in front will tend to come across the chest and the rear arm will drive backwards with the elbow at an angle of about 90°, but this angle changes throughout the forward and backward drive and should not be held mechanically always at the same angle.

At this point, it is useful to recall that as in other events, there is no **one** ideal style. Athletes differ in their body structure; their arm (and leg) levers are therefore different, and consequently styles will differ slightly.

Nevertheless, one must guard against a tiring, wasteful arm action, and against a shoulder/arm action that will tend to lift the feet off the floor. The hands are usually quite relaxed, playing little part in the drive. It must be remembered that an emphasis on arm drive can occasionally enable walkers with tired legs to increase speed.

It is important, therefore, to adopt a good arm style that can contribute to the drive forwards, prevent lifting of the feet, and assist in the hip-rotation process.

Training

For beginners, short distances are recommended: hikes, time trials, relay races, team races, etc. The emphasis should be on fun, adhering to the rules, getting used to the technique of race-walking, and avoiding the temptation to run.

When teachers or coaches are convinced that the athletes are ready for planned training, a systematic programme can be prepared. During the early stages, the emphasis will be on correct technique with the coach ensuring that the distances covered are not so long that the skill factor breaks down.

WALKERS
BEGINNER SCHOOLCHILDREN (Off-season)

DAY 1	Cover 3 miles with a mixture of walking and jogging, with the emphasis on style
DAY 2	No walking
DAY 3	On track or school field, walk 600m twice; walk 400m twice; walk 200m twice
DAY 4	No walking
DAY 5	Races with fellow pupils, relays, team races, etc.

WALKERS
BEGINNER SCHOOLCHILDREN (During season)

DAY 1	Walk 2 miles using three-quarters effort
DAY 2	No walking
DAY 3	Walk 600m, rest; walk 500m, rest; walk 400m, rest; walk 300m, rest; walk 200m, rest; walk 100m
DAY 4	No walking
DAY 5	Cover 3 miles with a mixture of walking and jogging
DAY 6	No walking
DAY 7	Competition: 1600m or 3000m

WALKERS
OLDER SCHOOLCHILDREN (Off-season)

DAY 1	Cover 5 miles with a mixture of fast and slow walking and jogging
DAY 2	Walk 2 miles, using three-quarters effort
DAY 3	Walk 800m twice; walk 400m three times; walk 200m four times
DAY 4	Walk 4 miles at a steady pace
DAY 5	No walking
DAY 6	Competition: 3000m or 5000m

WALKERS
OLDER SCHOOLCHILDREN (During season)

DAY 1	Cover 6 miles with a mixture of fast and slow walking and jogging
DAY 2	Walk 3 miles at a steady pace
DAY 3	Walk 400m fast; walk 200m slow; walk 400m fast; walk 200m slow Repeat sequence twice
DAY 4	Walk 4 miles at a steady pace
DAY 5	No walking
DAY 6	Competition: 3000m or 5000m

Juniors

As the children gain experience, the teacher or coach can check them for the ten main faults during at least one of the training sessions per week.

Faults:
1. Placing the front foot down flat
2. Placing the front foot down sideways
3. Leg not straight at the knee
4. Over-striding
5. Under-striding
6. Over-emphasis of the hip swing
7. The centre of gravity of the body bouncing up and down during the walk
8. Shoulder shrugging
9. Leaning forward with head or trunk
10. Leaning backwards with head or trunk

The checking and correction of these faults should be done with the coach standing well away from the athlete, and observing his or her progress from the side, front and back.

Additionally, winter training can include circuit training, weight training and endurance running on the track and over country courses.

JUNIOR WALKERS (Off-season)

DAY 1	Walk 8 miles at a steady pace
DAY 2	Do weight training or circuit training
DAY 3	5-mile Fartlek, including fast and slow walks and jogging
DAY 4	Walk 3 miles fast
DAY 5	Track running: run 800m twice; run 600m twice; run 400m twice
DAY 6	Walk 6 miles, working on technique
DAY 7	Rest day

JUNIOR WALKERS (During season)

DAY 1	Walk 6 miles at a steady pace
DAY 2	Walk 4 miles with a mixture of fast and slow walking
DAY 3	Walk 1000m five times
DAY 4	Walk 3 miles fast
DAY 5	Walk 800m twice; walk 600m twice; walk 400m twice; walk 200m twice
DAY 6	Rest day
DAY 7	Competition

Seniors

For those walkers who continue training beyond the junior stage, it can be assumed that they are sufficiently well-motivated to wish to train daily with a variety of types of work. A hard programme can therefore be planned, with the assurance that there has been a progressively developed style and background of fitness training.

The next stage of training can be specifically designed to eradicate the athlete's weaknesses and at the same time prepare him for the more energy-sapping longer distance races. The athlete will be expected to warm-up well before each daily session; to work daily on mobility exercises that will make him more supple in the joints and less tense in the muscles; to work hard on advanced weight-training techniques to improve his strength; to use circuit-training as an indication of improvement in his muscular endurance; and to improve his speed by training over shorter distances than his race distance whilst ensuring that his style is legal.

One of the important features of advanced training is that there should be plenty of variety to relieve the boredom of the constant hard work. This can be achieved by ensuring a mixture of track, road and country work, a mixture of indoor and outdoor work, a constant change of environment, a regular change of the distances covered, and, most important of all, an assurance that the work is progressively more difficult, of more volume and related to an athlete's improved strength and endurance as the year progresses.

Additionally, an advanced athlete will take greater care of his leisure hours, i.e. no smoking, no alcohol, no late nights, a good diet, meticulous care and cleanliness of clothing and body, and regular medical checks. In view of the long distances covered, particular attention should be paid to diet, bearing in mind the possible need for supplementary foods, drinks, vitamins—all in conjunction with medical advice and not taken because of a whim or a belief that patent medicines can improve performance. The advanced walkers will also consider the need for sustenance during their races, and will experiment with different drinks and foods during their training period, to ensure that on racing days they eat or drink only substances in which they have confidence.

At this stage of an athlete's career, he will be less inclined to want to take a few days rest should he have a sports injury. The treatment of sports injuries is not always the family doctor's province; in fact, the athlete himself can often educate the doctor about specific injuries related to his own event. Nevertheless, advanced walkers should be working in co-operation with family doctors, and where available, sports injuries specialists. Where there is an injury, some form of training can still be done—avoiding the particular muscle area in which the injury is present.

SENIOR WALKERS (Off-season)

DAY 1	Walk 15–20 miles across country and/or road
DAY 2	Do weight training or circuit training
DAY 3	Fartlek (cross-country running, fast and slow)
DAY 4	Walk using three-quarters effort for 2 hours
DAY 5	Short walk (30 minutes) plus weight training
DAY 6	Rest from walking (play games, basketball, badminton, etc.)
DAY 7	Competition or time trial

SENIOR WALKERS (During season)

DAY 1	Walk for 3 hours, using three-quarters effort
DAY 2	Run 200m eight times. Possibly some weight training
DAY 3	Walk 1600m twice; walk 1200m twice; walk 800m twice; walk 400m twice
DAY 4	Walk for 2 hours at a steady pace
DAY 5	Walk 600m three times; walk 400m three times; walk 200m three times; walk 100m three times FAST
DAY 6	30 minutes jogging and stretching exercises
DAY 7	Competition or time trial

Tactics

It is useful to plan races taking into account an athlete's present level of fitness, his strengths, his target (i.e. the position expected in the race, or a time), the opposition's strengths, weaknesses and abilities, and the nature of the course and weather. Unlike runners, walkers get no benefit from being shielded by the wind by walking behind someone else, neither is it always possible or advisable to change speed or put in spurts during the race. Such action is wasteful of energy and can lead to disqualification if illegal 'lifting' of the feet results.
It is therefore important that a walker knows his own ability and learns to appreciate at what speed he is walking at any time. Opponents might try to walk as fast as possible immediately the race begins; if an athlete attempts to match this, he could 'burn himself up'. Surprisingly, if he decides not to go off with the fast bunch at the start, but retains a speed he knows he can cope with, he might well be overtaking the others at a later point during the race when they become tired.
Nevertheless, it is useful during training to try a number of different speeds and speed changes to discover whether they suit the individual. It may well be that some walkers will discover that they are good uphill walkers; they will therefore ensure that they obtain maximum advantage from the uphill stages of a race. The psychological factor is also very important. Walkers should not be tempted to change their own styles or plans because of the performance of others. Changing of style or effort can lead to disqualification, especially in the latter stages of a race.

Rules

(a) Athletes must progress in such a way that unbroken contact with the ground be maintained.
(b) The Chief Judge plus one other judge may disqualify a competitor if the style of walking does not comply with the rules.
(c) A walker may be given one caution if his walking style is not a valid one.
(d) On disqualification, the competitor must immediately leave the track, or in a road race remove his number.
(e) Refreshments shall be provided in races of more than 20 kilometres at the 10 km point and every 5 km thereafter.

APPENDIX A
STANDARD ATTAINMENTS TO BE ATTEMPTED BY SCHOOLGIRLS

Girls' Sprints and Hurdles

	100 metres	200 metres	400 metres	Hurdles
Under 13 years	15.6 sec	—	—	15.0 sec (70m)
Under 14 years	15.1 ,,	32.5 sec	—	14.2 ,, (70m)
Under 15 years	14.7 ,,	31.4 ,,	—	14.4 ,, (75m)
Under 16 years	14.5 ,,	30.7 ,,	73.7 sec	15.8 ,, (80m)
Under 17 years	14.3 ,,	30.2 ,,	72.6 ,,	15.6 ,, (80m)
Under 18 years	14.2 ,,	29.8 ,,	71.7 ,,	15.9 ,, (100m)

Girls' Middle-Distance and Cross-country

	800 metres	Cross-country Distance
Under 13 years	3 min 08 sec	
Under 14 years	2 min 58 sec	Approximately 2,500 metres
Under 15 years	2 min 50 sec	
Under 16 years	2 min 47 sec	Approximately 3,000 metres
Under 17 years	2 min 45 sec	
Under 18 years	2 min 43 sec	Approximately 3,500 metres

APPENDIX B
STANDARD ATTAINMENTS TO BE ATTEMPTED BY SCHOOLBOYS

Boys' Sprints and Hurdles

	100 metres	200 metres	400 metres	Hurdles
Under 13 years	14.6 sec	31.0 sec	—	14.2 sec (70m)
Under 14 years	14.2 ,,	29.8 ,,	72.0 sec	14.5 ,, (75m)
Under 15 years	13.9 ,,	28.9 ,,	69.2 ,,	14.9 ,, (80m)
Under 16 years	13.6 ,,	28.2 ,,	67.2 ,,	18.1 ,, (100m)
Under 17 years	13.4 ,,	27.5 ,,	65.4 ,,	17.5 ,, (100m)
Under 18 years	13.2 ,,	26.8 ,,	64.1 ,,	20.4 ,, (110m)

Boys' Middle Distance and Steeplechase

	800 metres	1,500 metres	5,000 metres	Steeplechase
Under 13 years	—	—	—	—
Under 14 years	2 min 45 sec	—	—	—
Under 15 years	2 min 40 sec	5 min 32 sec	—	—
Under 16 years	2 min 34 sec	5 min 18 sec	—	6 min 00 sec (1,500m)
Under 17 years	2 min 30 sec	5 min 08 sec	—	5 min 46 sec (1,500m)
Under 18 years	2 min 26 sec	5 min 00 sec	18 min 48 sec	7 min 34 sec (2,000m)

Cross-country
Because of the different terrain included on different courses, no standard times are suggested, but the distances run should be as follows:
Aged 13 and 14 — under 3 miles
Aged 15 and 16 — under 4 miles
Aged 17 and 18 — under 6 miles
Aged 19 — under 10 miles

APPENDIX C
STANDARDS FOR SCHOOLCHILDREN IN ATHLETICS CLUBS

Targets for Schoolgirls in Athletics Clubs
i.e. additional coaching outside school

	100 metres	**200 metres**	**400 metres**	**800 metres**	**Hurdles**
Aged 13 & 14	14.0 sec	30.0 sec	—	2 min 40 sec	12.9 sec (70m)
Aged 15 & 16	13.0 ,,	27.5 ,,	64.0 sec	2 min 29 sec	13.5 ,, (80m)
Aged 17 & 18	12.9 ,,	26.9 ,,	62.5 ,,	2 min 25 sec	17.2 ,, (100m)
Aged 19	12.8 ,,	26.5 ,,	61.0 ,,	2 min 22 sec	16.1 ,, (100m)

Targets for Schoolboys in Athletics Clubs

	100 metres	**200 metres**	**400 metres**	**Hurdles**
Aged 13 & 14	13.1 sec	27.2 sec	62.0 sec	14.2 sec (80m)
Aged 15 & 16	12.0 ,,	23.8 ,,	55.0 ,,	15.6 ,, (100m)
Aged 17 & 18	11.7 ,,	23.4 ,,	53.2 ,,	16.7 ,, (110m)
Aged 19	11.6 ,,	23.0 ,,	51.0 ,,	16.2 ,, (110m)

	800 metres	**1,500 metres**	**5,000 metres**	**Steeplechase**
Aged 13 & 14	2 min 30 sec	5 min 08 sec	—	—
Aged 15 & 16	2 min 06 sec	4 min 21 sec	—	5 min 15 sec (1,500m)
Aged 17 & 18	2 min 02 sec	4 min 07 sec	—	6 min 30 sec (2,000m)
Aged 19	1 min 56 sec	3 min 55 sec	14 min 30 sec	9 min 50 sec (3,000m)

APPENDIX D
STANDARDS FOR WALKERS

Boys	1600 metres	3000 metres	5000 metres
Under 13	10 min 20 sec	—	—
Under 15	—	20 min	—
Under 16	—	19 min 30 sec	—
Under 17	—	19 min	—
Under 18	—	—	33 min
Under 19	—	—	32 min
Under 20	—	—	31 min

Girls	1600 metres	2000 metres	3000 metres
Under 15	10 min 30 sec	—	—
Under 17	—	14 min 15 sec	—
Under 20	—	—	23 min 20 sec

Further Reading

British Amateur Athletic Board, *Know the Game Athletics* (EP Publishing, 1976)
G. Dyson, *Mechanics of Athletics* (University of London Press, 1962)
English Schools' Athletics Association, *Handbook.*
A. Ward, *Modern Distance Running* (Stanley Paul, 1964)
N. Whitehead, *Conditioning for Sport* (EP Publishing, 1975)

Official publications of the Amateur Athletic Association can be obtained from 2 Burn Close, Oxshott, Leatherhead, Surrey